SHARING
JESUS

the Church's most urgent task

SHARING
JESUS

the Church's most urgent task

Rob Frost

TRIBUTE
EDITION
Foreword by
Andy Frost

'Rob Frost was a remarkable man. He had a passion for telling people about Jesus which was infectious and gave rise to a whole new dynamism in the Methodist Church where he was such a key figure.'

– Nicky Gumbel, Alpha

SHARING JESUS: published by Scripture Union, 207–209 Queensway, Bletchley, MK2 2EB, UK.

email: info@scriptureunion.org.uk

Internet: www.scripture.org.uk

SHARING JESUS was first published in 2000 as SHARING JESUS IN A NEW MILLENNIUM; this 2008 title is based on this material, substantially revised.

ISBN 978 1 844427 356 0

British Library Cataloguing-in-Publication Data: a catalogue record for this book is available from the British Library.

Cover design by David Lund Design & Advertising Ltd, Milton Keynes. Internal design and layout by Creative Pages: www.creativepages.co.uk Printed and bound in the UK by Butler and Tanner.

CONTENTS

Dedicated
to all those thousands of Christians
who have dared to share Jesus in the UK
and in different parts of the world.

Share Jesus INTERNATIONAL

Share Jesus International (SJI) is a mission charity
founded by the Rev Dr Rob Frost in 2001.

SJI works with a spectrum of Church denominations,
networks and organisations, communicating the
message of Jesus.

For many years SJI ran Easter People, a national conference
of over of 8,000 people; Share Jesus missions, working with
hundreds of local churches; and national tours celebrating
music and the arts including Hope and Dreams.

The work continues today with the Pentecost Festival and
numerous other mission projects.

For more details: www.sharejesusinternational.com

FOREWORD AND FAREWELL

I t was a blustery November evening when Rob passed into eternity. I stood in the quiet intensive care unit as my father, surrounded by complex machines and cables, breathed his last. It was a holy moment. Something of God touched our lives in the solemnity.

All the technical apparatus that surrounded his bed could not maintain his earthly existence. His spirit had left... his empty body was motionless... he had gone. But there was no doubt as to where he had gone. He was set for an eternity with his heavenly Father.

The reality of the situation brought home to me once again the truth of the gospel – the gospel that Rob had preached... the gospel that he had lectured on... the gospel for which he toured with vast casts and orchestras... the gospel he had made TV shows about... the gospel that he had written about in the pages of this book... this was the same gospel that carried him to be with his Maker.

In my father's last weeks, he lived with the reality of death almost as if he was in a departure lounge between this life and the full newness of life. During this time of soul-searching, he knew a greater sense of the promises of Jesus. These promises gave him a depth of peace during the sleepless nights and painful surgery.

Rob leaves a great legacy. His life was well lived because his life was focused not on the temporary but on what was eternal.

For the past six years, I have lived and worked alongside my father at Share Jesus International. They have not always been easy times. I never planned to work with my dad! But, over these years, my dad modelled to me what is really most important in life.

I have a vast array of memories of how we dreamed and schemed for the kingdom of God together. We both loved to think creatively and it was often at one in the morning, seasoned with prayer, when the best ideas would come to light. Over late-night cups of tea or good curries, we would cast vision and allow God to birth fresh inspiration.

Rob achieved great things. He pioneered massive touring productions from which Cliff Richard's 'Millennium Prayer' reached number one in the charts. He held massive televised services making the *News at Ten* with people such as Princess Diana. He travelled the globe speaking at prestigious conferences to thousands of people.

But the lasting legacy is not the big productions. The most important legacy he left is in people's individual lives. In the condolence cards lining the shelves and floor of our home as I write this, two messages repeatedly shine through. First of all, people have written simply to say 'thanks'. They share memories of how Rob introduced them to Jesus. Whether it was over a coffee or in a church gathering, God used Rob to introduce many people to Jesus. This ministry was not just about preaching Jesus from a platform but about taking everyday opportunities with the cabbie, the hairdresser and the person sitting next to him on the plane.

The other message that has come strongly through the messages of condolence is that many people discovered their call through Rob's work. Between appointments, Rob always had time for a chat with all sorts of people. He encouraged them to share their faith. He allowed people to step up into new things. And through his work many people have been mobilised into mission and evangelism.

In a world that is losing all understanding of who Jesus is, those of us who love and follow him have an unprecedented opportunity. No denomination, no ministry, no book and no personality can bring change in the way that meeting Jesus can transform people. As Rob communicates so passionately in this book, we need to return to our core charge: to share Jesus. The same great commission that catapulted the early Church into creating a revolutionary Jesus-sharing movement mobilised my father to action – and now releases me to see God's kingdom come.

The baton passes to another generation. God used Rob's surrendered life – and so God can use ours.  We need to let Rob's life well lived challenge us to be carriers of God's grace and mercy into the world. It's all about sharing Jesus – the core value that unpinned Rob's life and all that we have ever done as an organisation.

When people ask us, 'So, what do you do?' let there be no hiding. We share Jesus.

Andy Frost
January 2008

1

PRINCIPLES
OF
EVANGELISM

1

JESUS-CENTRED EVANGELISM

I was 21 and had invited a group of friends to join me on a beach mission in the Cornish surf resort of Newquay. It was a daunting experience and I was very nervous. On the second day, an elderly evangelist called Herbert Silverwood arrived unexpectedly. I was deeply moved that this man, almost 80, should come to spend time with me and the team on our first ever beach mission. He was known throughout the country as one of the most outstanding evangelists of his generation. I was even more amazed that he was willing to sleep on the floor in the church vestry! He obviously had an uncomfortable night because at breakfast the next morning he said, 'I had to get up in the night for a rest!'

It was great to have someone around who had been an evangelist for nearly 50 years, and I was constantly pumping him for tips on how to do evangelism well. His advice was always simple but profound. 'Tell them about Jesus,' he said. 'If you lift Jesus high, many will be drawn to him.'

Day after day I watched Herbert at work on the promenade at Newquay. By evening hundreds gathered to hear his amazing fund of jokes and hilarious experiences, all delivered in a broad Yorkshire accent. The holidaymakers loved it, and many stayed on while he went on to tell the familiar stories of Jesus in vivid detail. As he drew a meeting to a close, he would urge his audience to 'follow my Jesus, because he'll do you good!' Afterwards, he would linger to talk to everyone, from kids to octogenarians, from families to teenage hecklers. He never missed an opportunity to talk about Jesus or to speak of his love for him, yet it was all so spontaneous and natural. It was evident that Jesus was an integral part of Herbert's life.

Sadly, not all the Christians who join me on mission teams each year have Herbert's ability to talk about Jesus. They seem to have grown up in a church culture where Christ is rarely spoken of in a personal way. Some hardly know the story of Jesus, let alone how to communicate it effectively to people who know nothing about him. But true evangelism will only happen when Christians talk about Jesus in ways that make others want to know him for themselves.

What's more, the activity of evangelism has been devalued by many churches. They seem under the impression that the occasional outreach event, special week of activities or leaflet drop is evangelism. But that may not be what is really happening. They may actually only be advocating the social activities of their local fellowship or promoting their particular denomination. This isn't true evangelism! It is no more than a recruitment drive akin to something which might be undertaken by a golf club or bingo hall. The yardstick for true Christian evangelism is simply this: Are we telling others about our Saviour? Are we really sharing Jesus?

> **The activity of evangelism has been devalued by many churches.**

The uniqueness of Jesus

Right from the announcement of his birth, God made it clear that Jesus would be no ordinary man. The nature of his birth marked him out as very different, proclaiming him to be the Son of God and not the son of Joseph. While many people today will accept that Jesus was a great prophet, teacher or healer, they won't accept that he is the Son of God. Yet without appreciating this aspect of his character, they haven't even begun to understand who he is. The early Church was so concerned to emphasise this, they made belief in his Sonship their basic confession for baptism. Mark's Gospel underscores its importance by opening with the words, 'The beginning of the gospel of Jesus Christ, the Son of God…'

In the early years of this twenty-first century, I believe that the acknowledgement of Jesus as the Son of God is under greater threat than it has been for many centuries. In a multicultural and multi-faith society, there is growing pressure to embrace those from other faith communities. We should welcome this kind of dialogue; but there are some tenets of our faith which are non-negotiable – and that Jesus is the Son of God is one of them. This contention over Jesus' identity lies at the very heart of Christian faith, since only when we accept that Jesus is God and truly divine do we discover who God is and what God is like.

The relevance of Jesus

The task of the evangelist is to tell the story of Jesus, but to tell it in such a way that it relates to the lives of ordinary men and women. The challenge is to apply this story in ways that relate to people's search for meaning, and to their deep-rooted and personal felt needs. The longer I do the work of an evangelist, the more amazed I am at just how relevant the Jesus story is. Whatever people are facing, however they are feeling and whoever they are, there is always some aspect of the Jesus story that can speak directly to them. There are hundreds of angles the evangelist can use to bring the gospel to contemporary men and women, but I will list here just a few of them to illustrate my point.

The New Age Jesus

One of the greatest contributions of Celtic Christians to the richness of our spirituality is that they recognised Christ is *immanent* – permanently pervading creation and the whole of life. They grasped the wonder that Christ is not only over all but also *in* all. His presence suffuses the whole of creation and fills every aspect of it. Christ's involvement in creation began right from the very start of time. He is the one who envisioned the changing season, the scudding cloud, the delicate flower, the glowing sunset. He is the one who brought it all into being, who created it all for us to see.

> [Christ] is the image of the invisible God, the firstborn over all creation. For by him all things were created: things in heaven and on earth, visible

and invisible, whether thrones or powers or rulers or authorities; all things were created by him and for him.

Colossians 1:15,16

In a time of New Age spirituality, the Celtic view of Jesus may be surprisingly helpful in giving us opportunities to talk about Jesus in ways with which New Agers will connect. The New Age thesis that the divine is immanent in all things can offer a way in for us to present this view of Jesus, and we can build bridges by telling people about the one whose love infuses the planet.

The powerless Jesus

We live in a world in which many feel powerless and forgotten. But the story of Jesus can bring great strength and comfort to people feeling like this. Jesus was not born in a palace but a stable. He didn't grow up among kings and princes but as a refugee in Egypt. He didn't walk the corridors of power but the road to the cross. He wasn't wealthy or of high social status; instead he mixed with tax collectors and prostitutes. And this Jesus didn't just get alongside the powerless; he knew what it was himself to be marginalised by society.

Not only did Jesus identify with the powerless, he saw his ministry as one that would bring radical change to their situation, challenging the power structures of the world. At a synagogue in his home town of Nazareth, he used the words of the prophet Isaiah to underline this aspect of his mission:

'The Spirit of the Lord is on me,
    because he has anointed me
    to preach good news to the poor.
He has sent me to proclaim freedom for the prisoners
    and recovery of sight for the blind,
to release the oppressed,
    to proclaim the year of the Lord's favour.'

Luke 4:18,19

All through his earthly ministry Jesus challenged the powerful. The Romans demanded total allegiance to the emperor. The wealthy, land-owning Sadducees demanded allegiance to the status quo. The pious Pharisees demanded allegiance to the observance of ritual. But Jesus wouldn't side with any of them. He refused to support their claims – because his priority was the kingdom of heaven, not the kingdoms of the earth. His was a currency that dealt in sacrifice, humility and meekness, which threatened the established power structures, interest groups and political regimes of his day.

> 'You know that the rulers of the Gentiles lord it over them, and their high officials exercise authority over them. Not so with you. Instead, whoever wants to become great among you must be your servant, and whoever wants to be first must be your slave – just as the Son of Man did not come to be served, but to serve, and to give his life as a ransom for many.'
> Matthew 20:25–28

Jesus' own ministry was a demonstration of servanthood. It sometimes overwhelms me that the Lord of all creation came to earth 'in the very nature of a servant'. His life was lived in complete obedience to the will of his Father. This can speak poignantly to those who feel powerless, reassuring them that, whatever their circumstances, Jesus – bringer of good news to the poor – is with them just where they are.

The rejected Jesus
Jesus loved the world with a depth of compassion we can't begin to understand. His leap from heaven to earth was made at enormous personal cost and led to painful experiences of rejection.

He was even rejected by those people he grew up with. Going back to Nazareth, to the carpenter's shop, to his mother and brothers and the small close-knit community in which he'd been raised, he might have expected a hero's welcome. Maybe they'd put the flags out for the small-town boy made good. Not a bit of it! Instead, he met resistance and murderous hostility.

He was snubbed by the religious elite. When Simon, a Pharisee, invited Jesus to dinner (Luke 7), he didn't invite him to honour him, hear him or affirm him. He offered him none of the marks of hospitality that a Jewish host of the time would have offered his guests – there was no kiss of welcome, no ceremonial washing bowl, no neatly folded towel. Instead, Jesus met with cynicism and mockery. It seems that Simon invited Jesus to humiliate him!

He was rejected, too, by his fellow countrymen. I remember one evening at sunset, standing on the Mount of Olives, looking down over Jerusalem. It brought alive for me that moment when Jesus looked over that same city and wept:

> 'O Jerusalem! Jerusalem, you who kill the prophets and stone those sent to you, how often I have longed to gather your children together, as a hen gathers her chicks under her wings, but you were not willing.'
> Matthew 23:37

Jesus had an aching burden for the people of that great city. He knew their needs and wanted to embrace them with his love. These were not empty sentiments but the expression of one who lived entirely for others and who was feeling deep within himself the pain of their rejection of him.

And finally he was betrayed and abandoned by his closest friends, the ones he might have expected to stick by him through any danger. When the guards came to arrest him in the Garden of Gethsemane they were led there by one of his own disciples and all the others fled in terror, leaving him to face his enemies alone.

Over and over again, the story of Jesus is a story of rejection. He was born in a borrowed stable and buried in a borrowed tomb, and between the two he knew what it was to walk a lonely road. It's little wonder, then, that he was often the friend of the rejected and shrank from no one. He cared for crooks like Zacchaeus, those of dubious morality like the woman of Samaria, and outcasts like the ten lepers. He still comes alongside life's outcasts today. His story speaks powerfully to anyone who has tasted the bitter experience of abandonment and loneliness. His life teaches that through him we can find acceptance, healing and adoption into the family of God.

The Saviour Jesus

Jesus knew what it was to be human – to struggle with temptation, to wrestle with the will of God, to agonise over the cost of total obedience to the Father. He even knew hell, in one bleak moment of separation from God. There was no dark human experience he was not willing to go through as he made his painful pilgrimage to the cross. But as Jesus hung on the cross, taking on himself the sin of the world, he also became a sacrifice for us. His death is a profound mystery, yet ultimately it's the most momentous event in human history: God taking on our humanity and dying on our behalf. Jesus died that we might know the depth of nature of God's love. He died that he might reach down to where we are and lift us up into the Father's presence. This is the quality of his caring and the magnitude of his compassion. The story of Jesus, then, is a story of hope; a gospel of forgiveness; an opportunity for new beginnings. The story of Jesus is the story of someone who came to rescue us and set us free:

> For God so loved the world that he gave his one and only Son, that whoever believes in him shall not perish but have eternal life. For God did not send his Son into the world to condemn the world, but to save the world through him.
>
> John 3:16,17

No longer need we look to the future with despair or fear. No longer need we carry heavy burdens of guilt and failure. We can ask Jesus to save us, to forgive us and to bring us into the kind of beautiful relationship with God which really makes life worth living.

The risen Jesus

The story of Jesus is a story of personal renewal. Three days after his crucifixion, Jesus came back to life. He overcame sin and suffering; he defeated the power of evil; he broke the hold death has over us. Each of us is invited to share in his victory and to claim it personally. We are invited to live in the joy of his resurrection, no matter what we face. We should know his resurrection power as part of our everyday lives. It should fill us with hope and help us see that whatever struggles we experience here on earth, we go through them in the strength of the one who has gone before us.

> [Jesus]... endured the cross, scorning its shame, and sat down at the right hand of the throne of God. Consider him who endured such opposition from sinful men, so that you will not grow weary and lose heart.
> *Hebrews 12:2,3*

This has to be a relevant and timely message for the countless millions of ordinary men and women today who feel oppressed and beaten down by life.

Jesus the Judge

It is sobering to remember that when he returns at the end of time, Jesus will come as our Lord and our Judge. On that day we will each have to bow the knee to him and account for how we have lived our lives. It would be very convenient if we knew the date of his return! We could make sure that we had prepared ourselves to meet him. But, though his return is definite, the day and the hour remain God's secret.

Those of us who have only ever thought of Jesus as our Friend and Comforter would do well to remember that he is also our Judge, lest we fall into the trap of overfamiliarity and fail to develop the respect he is due as the one to whom we are ultimately accountable. Jesus himself stressed the importance of this accountability, making it clear that it is an essential part of our relationship with him:

> 'Moreover, the Father judges no one, but has entrusted all judgment to the Son, that all may honour the Son just as they honour the Father. He who does not honour the Son does not honour the Father, who sent him'.
> *John 5:22,23*

Many of us compartmentalise our lives to such an extent that judgement is seen as something in the future – distant, unreal, in another time and place. But Christ's judgement is not just destined for the end of history: it is ongoing, constant, *now*. If our lives are not at one with his life, we will feel the sharp sword of his judgement in our lives, our spirituality and our ministry, *now*:

> 'I am the vine; you are the branches. If a man remains in me and I in him, he will bear much fruit; apart from me you can do nothing. If anyone does not remain in me, he is like a branch that is thrown away and withers; such branches are picked up, thrown into the fire and burned.'
> John 15:5,6

Jesus is our Judge today and tomorrow; now and in eternity. This has to be a part of our message to a fun-loving, hedonistic society where 'live now, pay later' is the rule. We should not play it down. When we tell the story of Jesus, we are inviting people to make room in their lives for confession, repentance and a chance to make amends. Unpopular though such a message may sound, it is an integral part of who Jesus is and what we believe about him.

The evangelist's message

I used to believe in God as some vague cloud of power – mysterious, unknowable, distant. But when I discovered who Jesus is, I discovered the true God who is 'I am'. One of the great joys of becoming a Christian is that we come to know Jesus personally and are drawn into the presence of God through him. There are some days when the friendship of Jesus is very real to me: days when he shares my burdens and carries my load. And there are other days when I don't feel him near at all. But even then I claim his promise that he will never leave me nor forsake me:

> 'My sheep listen to my voice; I know them, and they follow me. I give them eternal life, and they shall never perish; no one can snatch them out of my hand.'
> John 10:27,28

As we seek to share the gospel with others, we must encourage them to listen for his voice among all the clamouring voices of the world we live in. There is much that will alarm us in this fast-changing and stressful society, but the voice of Jesus can still breathe its ancient peace into any situation. This is the voice they must know and follow, which will reassure them when things seem to be falling apart, and which will lead them to eternal joy at the end of this transient life. This is the voice whose Word rings true behind our words. When I'm briefing mission teams, I still repeat the advice of the old-time evangelist Herbert Silverwood: 'Tell them about Jesus! – because my experience has shown that even in a complex multicultural society, this is what they want to hear.'

> **... his voice can still breathe its ancient peace into any situation.**

Jesus strides across the centuries to us today to address our sense of confusion, loss of direction and lack of meaning. His call to us, as to every generation, is simply, 'I am the way'. This isn't primarily an invitation to follow his teaching or to adopt a set of theological precepts. He is inviting us to share a relationship with him. He welcomes us as friends. This single relationship will have the most profound effect on our lives. Jesus will transform our priorities and change our perspectives. More than that, as we allow him to take over our lives he will actually redeem us, releasing us from slavery to failure, sinfulness and selfishness. He will set us free. He will take our scars – the wounds that go deep into our past, the hurts, the disappointments, the regrets, the dark shadows that haunt us down the years – and heal them.

This is not a once-for-all experience. As we welcome Jesus into the different areas of our personality, we will see his ongoing work of redemption. In knowing him, loving him and communing with him, we discover that he meets those needs nothing else can meet; for he is the One who gave us life and to whom, one day, we must give account as to how we have lived it.

Jesus is at the centre of all we believe. He is what makes Christianity distinctive and is the reason behind our evangelism. For over 20 years I have led Share Jesus missions in hundreds of churches.

As I go out on mission, the project's title always reminds me of the purpose for my going. I must share Jesus, nothing more and nothing less. In sharing him, I share the heart of the gospel message. This has rarely been a matter of going through a theological formula. Rather, it has been an opportunity to introduce people to my best friend. Introducing them to the local church, the denomination or even the fellowship of local Christians is always secondary.

For far too long the word 'evangelism' has been a dirty word in the life of the Church.

For far too long the word 'evangelism' has been a dirty word in the life of the Church. We have talked 'mission', we have talked 'service' and we have talked 'political action', but many church leaders have avoided the evangelistic task Jesus commissioned us all to undertake. Statisticians tell us that most churches spend less time talking about it, spend less money on it and expend less energy on it than almost anything else they do. Postmodernism, with its emphasis on connecting with our roots and on being real about what we believe, poses many new challenges. But perhaps, above all, it gives us a wonderful opportunity to put evangelism back at the top of the agenda.

2

SPIRIT-FILLED EVANGELISM

Some years ago I visited Pensacola in Florida, where there has been a powerful move of the Holy Spirit in recent times. Hundreds of thousands of people have given their lives to Christ, and thousands have experienced the renewal of the Holy Spirit in powerful ways.

While the focus of the revival has been the Assemblies of God church in one of the inner-city areas of Pensacola called Brownsville, the Methodist Church in the suburbs at Pine Forest has also been deeply touched by this move of the Spirit.

The young people from the youth group of this church were the first to attend the Brownsville revival meetings, but soon they dragged their parents along. Finally, Perry Dalton, the United Methodist pastor, went downtown to see what all the fuss was about! His own ministry was changed and renewed and he began to call the local Methodist congregation to fasting and prayer. They in their turn were touched by the Holy Spirit, and this led to a painful and powerful time of confession, repentance and forgiveness. Families were brought together, marriages healed, parents and children reunited, and many deep pastoral situations brought out into the open for ministry through prayer and counselling. It wasn't all good news, however. About one third of the congregation resigned their membership in protest at the change of emphasis and direction of their church. As they left, many others – particularly those on the fringes of church life – came to take their place.

I made two visits to Pine Forest, and on both occasions my own life was deeply challenged and my ministry renewed. Preaching there in the 1990s, I was fascinated to discover that they still had quite a traditional form of worship. There was a choir, robed altar boys and a liturgical format. When I announced the first hymn and people stood up to sing, the presence of the Holy Spirit was almost tangible. By the second verse, four people were kneeling at the altar rail in floods of tears, wanting to confess their sins and get right with God. By the time I started to preach, the altar rail was full and the prayer team was at work among them. I turned to the pastor and asked if I should go on. He urged me to do so and, as I continued, yet more of the congregation came forward in repentance.

While there are many aspects of such a revival that I personally struggle with, and certain phenomena which bother me, I am left with one overwhelming emotion. If the Holy Spirit can renew a fairly traditional United Methodist Church in suburban Florida, he can do it anywhere!

Perhaps we have sanitised the Holy Spirit and made him too safe. Perhaps we prefer that he remain under control rather than have free rein among us. Perhaps the form of Christianity found in many of our churches needs his refreshing power to shake us up and remind us whose Church it really is!

There was certainly nothing safe about the first Pentecost. Luke describes the arrival of the Spirit as like the 'blowing of a violent wind' which rushed through the house in which the disciples were meeting:

> They saw what seemed to be tongues of fire that separated and came to rest on each of them. All of them were filled with the Holy Spirit and began to speak in other tongues as the Spirit enabled them.
> Acts 2:3,4

Scary stuff! Imagine the reaction of your local congregation if this happened on Sunday. Wow! Imagine it happening at your parish council, elders meeting or leaders committee?

Having experienced Pine Forest United Methodist Church for myself, these things don't seem as impossible as they once appeared. But why would God do this? Why would he send the Holy Spirit to 'zap' us in these new ways? Well, I don't believe he does it to give us a warm glow inside. I don't think he does it just to give us a Pentecostal experience. And I don't think he does it to get us dancing in the aisles! No. The Bible makes it clear that when God sends the Holy Spirit, he sends him for mission and to empower his people.

❖ Jesus told his disciples that as the Father had sent him so he was sending them; then he breathed on them, telling them to receive the Holy Spirit. He was giving them power to fulfil the great commission, to 'go and make disciples of all nations'.

❖ On the day of Pentecost, when the disciples received the Holy Spirit, it wasn't followed by a seven-day revival convention. No. Immediately they began to communicate in the languages of the people gathered in Jerusalem, and to speak the gospel in ways that could be understood. He was giving them power to communicate.

❖ When the early Church was looking for a group of people to engage in a work of practical ministry to care for those in need among them, what did they look for? Seven men 'known to be full of the Spirit and wisdom' (Acts 6:3). He gave them power to act.

What has all this to do with evangelism in the church today? Well, many local churches are struggling to fulfil the mission God has given us. If we want to be really effective in evangelism, we need to wait on God for the renewing power of the Holy Spirit. We need to recognise that we cannot do this work in our own strength, and to admit that many of our strategies aren't really working because they lack God's anointing on them.

The Holy Spirit at work in evangelism

Some years ago I visited Niagara Falls on the border between the United States and Canada. At the time it was possible to take a trip into the caves behind the Falls and to experience the thundering power of the water close up. I got togged up in a waterproof suit and edged my way behind the guide into the network of cavernous passages behind this massive waterfall. Eventually we arrived in a small chamber directly behind the centre of Niagara Falls.

The roar was deafening and a fine sheet of spray filled the space where we were. Rainbows danced in the sunlight on every side. It was spectacular to look through the roaring torrent of water just a few metres away.

Since 1961 the Niagara project has been generating electricity. In 2006 a massive upgrade made it the biggest electricity producer in New York State, generating 2.4 million kilowatts – enough power to light 24 million 100-watt light bulbs at once!

As I stood watching the waterfall from the cavern, its power almost tangible around me, I began to think of the power of the Holy Spirit, which shaped the universe and brought creation out of chaos. Niagara Falls, by comparison, pales into insignificance! I began to look on the Holy Spirit in a different way. If he has the power to hold the cosmos together and to keep the planets swirling in their rightful orbit, what an enormous waste it is not to use that power to equip us for the task of evangelism!

> **Too much evangelism is done in the power of human personality and creativity, and not enough is done in the power of God.**

Too much evangelism is done in the power of human personality and creativity, and not enough is done in the power of God. Too much evangelism ends up weak and ineffectual because it has failed to draw on the resources of the Holy Spirit. Yet it is his ministry we are engaging in; it is his task to convict men and women of sin and thus begin the process of conversion. The part we play is simply enabling people to discover his renewing and transforming power in their lives.

The apostle Paul makes it clear that the Holy Spirit is active in the ongoing development of our relationship with God. A quick review of what he writes in Romans chapter 8 shows that through the Holy Spirit:

❖ We are set free from the law of sin and death. Without the help of the Holy Spirit we are powerless to do anything outside of our sinful nature (verses 1–4).

❖ Our minds begin to tune in to what God wants. Through the activity of the Holy Spirit we are able to overcome the power of sin with all its deadly effects (verse 5).

❖ We discover the daily life which God wants us to enjoy. Only by the Spirit of God can we have victory over temptation and evil in our lives. In fact, without the Holy Spirit we cannot even belong to Christ (verses 6–9).

❖ We receive the guarantee of eternal life and know that the day will come when we will rise to live with Christ forever. But eternal life is not just for the future; it is an experience that begins when we follow Christ (verses 10,11).

❖ We know how to live and what to do. The Spirit witnesses to the fact that we are God's children and gives us the confidence to approach him as 'Abba, Father' (verses 12–17).

How can we possibly engage in evangelism without recognising that it is the Holy Spirit's work? Evangelism is no more than us coming into partnership with him as he continues to do what he is already doing in people's lives. If we try to do evangelism without him, we will find it so much harder. We need the Spirit's power if we are to communicate with those who are blinded by the 'god of this age'. Even more, we need his discernment and authority if we are to break down spiritual strongholds and set people free:

> For though we live in the world, we do not wage war as the world does. The weapons we fight with are not the weapons of the world. On the contrary, they have divine power to demolish strongholds.
> *2 Corinthians 10:3,4*

It has always fascinated me that during the industrial revolution the entrepreneurs of eighteenth-century Britain were able to discover different sources of power and use them for many purposes. I came across one small area near Manchester in which there had sprung up a snuff mill, a flour mill, a cotton mill and several other industrial factories. They were all driven by the same small river.

It is God's power – the Holy Spirit – which should drive and energise all activity in Christ's name. If we try to do evangelism in our own strength, we are wasting the power God has made available to us. How ludicrous that we should even think of engaging in evangelism without working with the creative power of God! How strange that we should try to evangelise without the Spirit whose work it really is! How ridiculous that we should try to evangelise without using the driving force he has given specifically for the task!

The Holy Spirit at work in the Church

Before his Ascension, Jesus instructed his disciples to wait in Jerusalem until they had received the promised power of God. This power was given so that they could fulfil his commission to go into all the world to make new followers.

One of the hallmarks of a group of believers who are empowered by the Holy Spirit is the quality of their life together. The early Church in Jerusalem gives us a clear example:

❖ The Christians in Jerusalem were known for friendship and willingness to share everything with one another; and for their concern for others.

❖ They were known for their ability to bring people to Christ, and for their effectiveness in looking after those new converts and drawing them into the life of the Church.

❖ The Jerusalem Christians had a strong sense of unity and a powerful prayer life.

❖ They did not tolerate sinfulness.

❖ They were committed to the growth and development of new work.

❖ Many believe that the Church in Jerusalem grew by thousands of people in the early months of its existence. This growth was surely a witness to its health as a fellowship.

The Jerusalem Christians were truly effective in evangelism because theirs was a Church empowered by the Spirit. Their life together paints a vivid picture of what a truly evangelistic group of Christians should look like.

The Holy Spirit in power evangelism

Jesus ushered in the kingdom of God by demonstrating his authority over the supernatural world, disease and death. He cast out demons, healed those who were sick, made the blind see, the lame walk and the deaf hear. He commanded nature's obedience by stilling the storm and walking on water. He raised dead people to life. Likewise, the apostles were known not only for their preaching and good works but also for their ability to perform miracles and thus demonstrate that the power of God really works. In Philip's ministry, we see this clearly illustrated:

> When the crowds heard Philip and saw the miraculous signs he did, they all paid close attention to what he said.
> Acts 8:6

Power evangelism relies on direct intervention by God in the lives of ordinary people. It recognises God's sovereign ability to break into our world with signs and wonders and miracles. John Wimber once commented, 'In pragmatic evangelism we say something and God acts, but in power evangelism God says something and we act' (*Power Evangelism*, Hodder & Stoughton, 1986). In this kind of outreach, demonstration and proclamation go hand in hand.

In my travels around the world I have come across many situations in which power evangelism has been mightily used by God: incredible healings, the miraculous arrival of rain, the dramatic conversion of violent criminals. I have not seen much power evangelism at work in my own ministry, and have sometimes wondered what kind of effect miraculous events would have in such a cynical secularised culture as the one in which we live in the UK.

I was deeply challenged by the testimony of a newly retired secondary school headmaster in a tough area of London. He confessed to me that he only really discovered that prayer works towards the end of his teaching career. He had become bored and fed up with a form of Christianity which seemed to lack credibility and power, so he started to 'put God to the test'. He told of incident after incident during the stressful years of leading a large school community when he dared to pray for miracles and told his staff and students that he was doing so. It was little wonder, therefore, that when his prayers began to be answered in the lives of individuals and of the whole community, people began to listen to him. They became hungry to know more about 'faith that works'!

The Holy Spirit in renewal and revival

Some Christians argue that we don't need evangelism; we need revival. They look to God to 'do the job for us' and 'bring the people back to Church'. Sadly, I fear that many of them don't really understand the nature of revival. Historically, revival is about what happens in the Church before anything can happen in the world!

AW Tozer, twentieth-century American preacher, pastor and author, pointed out that many churches needed revival. The telltale signs of this need were, in his opinion, 'rut, rote and rot'. There are many such church groups around today. They are lacking direction; religious but without any sense of understanding or reality in their faith. They expect nothing to happen and have no vision for reaching the lost.

The famous Dr Martyn Lloyd-Jones once preached:

> We can define revival as a period of unusual blessing and activity in the Church. A revival is something that happens first in the Church and among Christian people. When the life of a church begins to wane, to droop and has almost become moribund it needs revival! Revival means awakening, stimulating the life, bringing it to the surface again. It happens primarily in the Church of God.

There are countless examples down the centuries of the reviving power of the Holy Spirit touching the lives of ordinary Christians and empowering them to evangelise the world. Let me just mention just a few.

The 100-year prayer meeting

In 1722, a small group of Christians in Germany met on the estate of Count Nikolaus von Zinzendorf. There they encountered the Holy Spirit in a powerful way. Their hearts were set aflame with a new love for Jesus Christ and for one another. They began to meet in prayer more regularly and on 25 August 1727 they established a round-the-clock prayer meeting which ran, uninterrupted, for a hundred years. At every moment of the day and night there were people praying. Out of this was born a mission to evangelise many unreached peoples. Tens of thousands of people became Christians through the ministry of these evangelists.

The warmed heart

On 1 January 1739, John Wesley and about sixty of his fellowship were praying deep into the night. He wrote in his diary:

> About three in the morning, as we were continuing constant in prayer, the power of God came mightily upon us, insomuch that many cried out for exceeding joy and many fell to the ground. As soon as we were recovered a little from that awe and amazement at the presence of His majesty we broke out with one voice – 'We praise Thee, O God, we acknowledge Thee to be the Lord.'

As a result of this empowering, and the 'strangely warmed heart' of John Wesley, revival flooded across the United Kingdom.

The one million converts in the US

In 1857, Jeremiah Lanphier gave out handbills in New York inviting fellows Christians to join him in prayer for the nation. On September 23 that year, just six people took up his invitation. A week later twenty came; the following week forty. The meetings grew so popular that he had to hold them daily. Within five months there were three prayer meetings happening simultaneously in large theatres in the city. Within a few months similar gatherings for prayer were happening in Boston, Chicago, Washington, Buffalo and Newark. Thousands gathered each day to pray for the spiritual renewal of the United States. In Portland, Oregon, the meetings grew so popular that 240 major stores closed each day between eleven in the morning and two in the afternoon to enable their employees to pray. Natural and spontaneous evangelism flowed from the tens of thousands of Christians caught up in this renewal of faith. Historians estimate that there were over one million new converts to Christ in 1858–59!

The one million converts in the UK
Meanwhile, in the United Kingdom, Charles Haddon Spurgeon was not only teaching about prayer, he was modelling the truth that prayer is integral to evangelism. Wherever he went, he called the Church to prayer, teaching that it was the springboard for all true mission and ministry. Whenever guests visited him at his church, the Metropolitan Tabernacle in London, he would show them the prayer room where church members kept up a 24-hour unceasing vigil of prayer. Out of this renewed sense of commitment to prayer in the churches arose a great wave of evangelistic activity. Church historians estimate that there were around one million new converts to Christianity in Britain during 1860 alone. New leaders who emerged from this revival time included Lord Shaftesbury, George Muller and William Booth.

Revival in the Philippines
Following five years of dedicated prayer by a small group of missionaries in the Philippines, retired pastor Paul Holsinger called the people of his church to repentance and reconciliation. The congregation was suddenly and powerfully renewed with the Holy Spirit and, as a result, hundreds of local townspeople were converted to Christianity. The revival swept from town to town. Even now, decades later, there is incredible church growth all across that region.

Revival in Korea

In Korea, possibly the best known example of contemporary revival, experts suggest that 110,000 of the population were converted in 1982, and 120,000 in 1983. Pastor Yonghi Cho, leader of one of the fastest growing 'super-churches' in the region, said, 'We have seen the importance of developing and keeping a prayer life. If we stop praying the revival will wane. If we continue praying, I believe that all Korea can be saved!'

In the UK, sporadic and limited bursts of revival have continued to the present day, particularly among the travelling gypsy populations and among prisoners. Overseas we hear of waves of renewal sweeping across the Church, affecting huge numbers of people in places like Toronto and Pensacola. God seems to be breaking down the structures of formalised institutional religion and inviting his people to meet him in new and uncluttered ways through miraculous demonstrations of his power.

I believe there will be many more waves of spiritual renewal in this century, each one calling us to move beyond the familiar trappings of our comfortable Christianity to meet God face to face. It is this kind of spiritual renewal that will enable ordinary people to discover the spiritual reality they crave and empower them to share the message in new ways that are both relevant and creative.

A number of common factors can be found in these great periods of growth in Christianity. Each seems to have been preceded by the raising up of groups to pray. Each seems to have brought forward young leaders with a heart for evangelism: people in the 1700s like George Whitfield (aged 22), Howell Harris (25) and John Wesley (36). Each manifests a renewed search for holiness, a mass movement in prayer, the re-emergence of authoritative biblical preaching and the introduction of new and radical methods of outreach and evangelism.

There is always, of course, a danger of feelings getting the upper hand. The eighteenth-century established Church was united in its suspicion of 'enthusiasm' – a term that meant much the same as 'fanatic' today – which they applied to anyone whose practice of

Christianity manifested any fervour. Such religion was considered to be a threat to the peace of the realm. They preferred religion to be quietly dispassionate. John Wesley, opposing the dependence on reason his Anglican contemporaries so advocated, also recognised the danger of relying too much on feelings. Wesley chose instead a middle way, one that expressed an awesome respect for the Bible, but interpreted in the light of reason, Church tradition and personal experience. His evangelistic fervour and advocacy of 'the strangely warmed heart' challenged the cold deism of the established Church, but he fiercely protected his followers from the fanaticism England had seen in the previous century.

> **Without the power of the Holy Spirit, evangelism is impossible; without prayer, evangelism is a waste of time.**

Similarly, Church leaders today must guard the flock lest feelings become more important than the teaching of the Bible. While twenty-first century society may hunger for miraculous demonstrations of God's power, we must ensure that these are based on the unchanging and eternal facts of the gospel of Jesus Christ.

Without the power of the Holy Spirit, evangelism is impossible; without prayer, evangelism is a waste of time. This is God's work and it would be presumptuous and futile to imagine we can do it without him.

3

GOD-GUIDED EVANGELISM

In the last two chapters we have seen that our message should be Jesus-focused and our methods Spirit-anointed. The third foundational principle about evangelism is that our motivation should be God-centred.

Our heavenly Father sees the big picture. He knows history from before the start of time to after its close. He understands us better than we understand ourselves. He is working his purposes out in ways far beyond our comprehension. In doing evangelism, we become partners in an activity God undertakes through us – and it can happen any time, anywhere and with anyone.

Any time

It was a dark, wintry afternoon and the snow was cascading down. I was out on pastoral visits in the mining village where I was a local minister. I had spent three hours visiting the sick and the elderly, and it was nearly time to go home. It was my last visit of the afternoon. I swallowed the strong brew of tea, and replaced the fragile cup and saucer on the table. I said my goodbyes to the old lady and trudged through the snow to my car. I had finished my visiting list; I was ready for a break.

The roads were treacherous; the wheels on my car slithered as I set off. It was clear we were in for a bad night. At the end of the road I got a strong feeling that I should go and visit an particular man. However, I felt very tired and I had another meeting later in the evening. I stopped the car, pulled the handbrake on, leaned back and sighed. I really didn't want to bother. I sat and analysed my feelings.

I wondered if I was going mad to have this strong compulsion about the visit. Maybe I was overtired, or affected by some guilt complex. Or maybe God really was trying to tell me something. Yet, this old man didn't really need a visit. He was quite well and surely wouldn't expect me to call on such a snowy afternoon.

Several minutes passed as I tried to reach a decision. At last I gave in. Instead of turning left towards home, I turned right toward the man's house. By now the snow was falling in great white clumps, and the car laboured as I drove up the steep hill toward the council estate where he lived. Having parked, I went through the gate and round to knock on the back door, as was the custom in our mining village.

The old man greeted me warmly and put the kettle on. Soon I was drinking yet another cup of hot strong tea. We talked about many things and I ended by sharing my faith about Jesus. I prayed for the old man before I left. I went home, wondering why I'd been to see him. It made no sense at all and I felt a little resentful that my free time before the evening meeting had been cut so short.

Late that night, however, the old man died unexpectedly of a heart attack. I was one of the last people to speak to him. If I hadn't trusted my gut feeling and gone to visit him, I think I'd have lived the rest of my life with a tinge of regret.

I am sure God guides us. If we are really listening to him and are sensitive to his prompting, he will help us to be in the right place at the right time, saying the right thing. Over the years I have come to realise that God-centred evangelism may mean a call to action at the most inconvenient moments. God has sometimes overturned my list of priorities, interrupted my social life or made me late for important engagements. He has sometimes had to overrule my diary or my schedule so that he can lead me into situations that are ripe for evangelism. His will doesn't always fit neatly with my plans!

If we really want to be effective in evangelism, we must be willing to say 'any time' to the Lord, and that means taking down the barriers around our schedule and letting him be Lord of all our time. Sadly, there are many Christians who fence off areas of their lives from the sovereign will of God, who have never made the connection between evangelism and their life. But Jesus made it clear that commitment to him was not easy and that following him may involve us in costly decisions:

> 'If anyone would come after me, he must deny himself and take up his cross daily and follow me. For whoever wants to save his life will lose it, but whoever loses his life for me will save it.'
>
> *Luke 9:23*

There is a great freedom in giving all our time to God. Suddenly we are available to be used in situations we might previously have considered unlikely fields for evangelism. The story of Philip and the Ethiopian official convinces me of the importance of submitting my plans and activities to God's guiding. Philip was in the middle of his big mission in a city in Samaria. The days had been packed with action, with large crowds at the meetings, miraculous signs, amazing healings and hundreds coming to Christ. The whole community had been influenced by the mission and 'there was great joy in that city' (Acts 8:8). Here was fertile ground for serving the Lord and furthering the gospel. Philip might well have wondered if it could be bettered! Then 'an angel of the Lord said to Philip, "Go south to the road – the desert road – that goes down from Jerusalem to Gaza."'

It must have seemed a comedown, standing by that desert road in the middle of nowhere. Philip may have wondered what he could possibly achieve. Surely staying in Samaria would have been a better use of his time? But just then, over the horizon, came a chariot carrying an Ethiopian treasury official – one man struggling to understand the Scriptures. At once Philip saw the purpose of his journey, but still it must have seemed rather mundane after the signs and wonders of his city mission. Nevertheless, he went ahead and did what he felt God was asking him to do: he got alongside the man, 'began with that very passage of Scripture and told him the good news about Jesus'. The outcome was immediate and positive: the Ethiopian accepted the gospel and was baptised. But that was all Philip was to see: 'the Spirit of the Lord suddenly took Philip away, and the eunuch did not see him again, but went on his way rejoicing' (Acts 8:39).

God-centred evangelism puts God on the throne and us at his service. When we engage in God-centred evangelism, we are not doing something special: we are only fulfilling what he expects of us. Of course, this style of Christian living is costly. Yet it opens us up to being in the centre of the Lord's will. When we allow each day to be fully his, we ourselves become fully his. At last we can honestly say to the Lord that we are wholly available.

There are some teachers you never forget. When I was a teenager, one of my college lecturers was a tall, bearded man with an unapproachable manner. He was always reciting his favourite motto: 'You have all of my sympathy, but none of my time.' He lived by what he said. It was hard to talk to him because he was always rushing off somewhere. I didn't want his sympathy, but I often needed a few moments of his time. Sadly, he was always too busy.

I'm sure that many of us have so filled our lives with 'important' activities that we are not available to respond to God's call. Day after day we rush from one place to the next, offering everyone we meet 'all of our sympathy but none of our time'. Some of us are moving through life at such a speed that we meet people but don't get to know them. We hear people but don't listen to them. We look at people but don't see their need. We miss opportunities for evangelism with those around us. We say to the Lord, 'Any time – but not just now!' The Lord sends people into our lives for many reasons but, sadly, we sometimes regard them as 'interruptions' to our busy schedule. In doing so, we are missing out on wonderful opportunities for witness. We have not discovered the joy and excitement of engaging in God-centred evangelism.

> **God-centred evangelism puts God on the throne and us at his service.**

Anywhere

One of my college mates used to say, 'Here comes Rob, always in the wrong place at the wrong time.' He meant it as a joke, but there was a sharp edge to what he said as well! If we are to engage in God-centred evangelism, we must allow him to put us where we can be properly useful to him. A crucial part of our Christian commitment is to say, 'Anywhere you send me, Lord, I will go.' For some people, that kind of commitment will mean a move to the other side of the world; for others, it will mean staying just where they are.

This is vividly illustrated by the story of Jonah. He certainly had to learn this lesson the hard way. When God asked him to go and preach to the people of Nineveh, he didn't want to go. Nineveh was a pagan city and he knew he wouldn't be welcome there. So Jonah decided on a compromise. He agreed to uproot and travel overseas, but he would choose the location. So he set sail for Tarshish. However, he didn't stop to think through the consequences: that by stepping out of the Lord's will, he would end up in the wrong place at the wrong time and be totally ineffective.

What happened next? The boat hit stormy weather, and Jonah was thrown into the sea and swallowed by a great fish. There, in the belly of the fish, he asked God for forgiveness and offered himself totally. God forgave him, and Jonah went to prophesy in the place God had ordained for his mission. It certainly wasn't an easy assignment – perhaps it wasn't what he would have planned for himself – but it was God's place. And, because he was in the right place at the right time, God blessed his ministry there:

> The Ninevites believed God. They declared a fast, and all of them, from the greatest to the least put on sackcloth ...
>
> When God saw what they did and how they turned from their evil ways, he had compassion and did not bring upon them the destruction he had threatened.
>
> *Jonah 3:5–10*

We cannot plan our own lives in the Lord's service. We cannot choose the opportunities *we* think are best, or the places *we* think are right. We must actively seek God's will and submit ourselves to it if we want to be effective in his service.

To be in the right place at the right time may involve us in pain or persecution. God's will for our lives does not always mean an easy time; in fact it may lead us into very difficult situations. This was highlighted for me when I visited a small town in Eastern Europe during the days of the cold war when Communism still reigned. It was good to meet the Christians there and to work with the local minister for several weeks; good, too, to be away from the tourist track and to sample the everyday life of the townspeople. The minister spoke fluent English, so he was able to act as interpreter. Through him I talked for hours with the local Christians. One group of teenagers told me about the subtle forms of persecution they encountered. Some found it impossible to get a grant for college because they were Christians; others talked of closed career prospects and trouble with the authorities. I was impressed by their strong faith and their willingness to stay faithful to Jesus Christ, whatever the cost. I wished that some of my youth group could hear them talk.

A little later I met an elderly minister. 'The trouble is,' he said, 'you have many young believers in the West, but I don't think their faith is very strong. Would they still follow Jesus if they had to pay the cost that our young people pay?' I looked at his drawn face and asked him if he'd ever thought of leaving his country and coming to serve Christ in the West. He seemed hurt by my suggestion and paused to think through his reply. Then he bent forward and with piercing eyes asked, 'What would happen to the sheep if all the shepherds ran away?'

For my friend in Eastern Europe, being in the right place meant staying just where he was. It would have been easy to run away to an easier climate and a ministry under less pressure. It can sometimes be harder to stay put for God. If we want to engage in God-centred evangelism, we must be willing to go anywhere to serve him – be it down the street or across the world. If we are open to his call, we can't put limits on where he might send us. In every season of our lives and every day of our busy schedule, our prayer must be, 'Lord, let me be in the right place at the right time.'

Anyone

I fumbled for the keys to the minibus. It was dark and pouring with rain. The gang of teenage lads was getting restless. I opened the rear door and let them in. They had been quite well behaved during the youth meeting but now they were in high spirits. It was time to head for home. We drove away from the Hackney church into the stream of London traffic.

The journey back to Deptford wasn't an easy one. My passengers seemed determined to make it memorable! They rocked the minibus from side to side, made rude faces out of the rear window and sang bawdy songs at the top of their voices. I soon reached the limits of my patience, so I pulled onto the verge and gave them a stern warning: they could either shut up or start walking! On we went through the Rotherhithe tunnel and along the dark South London streets. As we drew up outside the church in Deptford where I worked, I sighed with relief.

Just as I was letting my passengers out, the caretaker burst through the church doors. 'You lot are in big trouble! You've really done it now!' he told us. 'If you're not all back in Hackney in thirty minutes, you'll have to face the police.'

The young people let out a loud groan of disapproval. I turned the vehicle round and headed back towards Hackney. An air of gloom descended on the group as they all fell silent.

Walter, the Hackney minister, greeted us at the church door. 'Look, lads,' he explained. 'There's a wallet gone missing and an old man is very upset because it contained his money and his pension book. A joke's a joke. Let's have it back and the matter need go no further.'

There was an uneasy silence. The lads looked at each other as they tried to work out whether to speak or keep silent. The silence continued for several minutes, then one of them said, 'It's in the gent's toilet – third cistern along. We didn't mean anything by it.'

Walter went off and returned a few minutes later with the dripping wallet held high. The lads apologised, if rather half-heartedly, and Walter beamed at us.

As the group boarded the minibus again, I went back to say sorry. I felt responsible. I was really fed up. Perhaps I should close the youth club down. It all seemed such a pointless waste of time.

Walter took one look at me and roared with laughter. 'Why on earth are you looking like that? This is nothing! You should see some of the scrapes I've landed myself in. I've spent most of my ministry chasing badly behaved kids around church premises. But that's what it's all about. The minute we stop caring for kids like these, we might as well give up!'

I knew he was right and over the years I've remembered his advice when I've been in worse situations. It isn't easy to care for young people who vandalise church premises, who prefer clubbing to conversation, who disappear whenever you need their help. It really saddens me when I hear of youth leaders or of churches who have given up on their young people. They've turned their backs on a great opportunity for evangelism and witness. Only recently I heard that a youth club was closed down because a mirror had been broken. The church council ruled that these youngsters were no longer welcome on church premises because they 'broke too much, didn't pay enough, and were too badly behaved'. They had closed the door on an important opportunity for God-centred evangelism.

Being realistic, we all find it hard to get on with some people. They may not have the same interests as us or they may just see things very differently. Sometimes when we open the front door to someone like that, it's hard to appear pleased to see them. The temptation is to make some excuse and get rid of them as quickly as we can. It can be costly to say, 'Anyone you send, Lord, I will love and be a witness to', for he may just ask us to serve those who have hurt us deeply or even scarred our lives. But Jesus taught that we should love our enemies and pray for those who persecute us:

> 'If you love those who love you what reward will you get? Are not even the tax collectors doing that? And if you greet only your brothers, what are you doing more than others? Do not even pagans do that?'
> Matthew 5:46,47

Ananias was a man willing to reach out and forgive, no matter what the cost. He was a committed Christian living in Damascus and a good witness for the Lord. One day he heard that Saul of Tarsus, the enemy of the Church, was on his way to town. This proud Jew was coming to break up the Church and throw all the Christians into jail. A terrifying prospect!

Then Ananias felt the Lord calling him to go to witness to Saul. It must have seemed like God was asking rather a lot – after all, such a meeting could cost Ananias his life. It would probably have been wiser to go into hiding until Saul left town. But Ananias obeyed and went to the house where Saul was staying. His knees must have been knocking as he went in! Yet the first words Ananias spoke were, 'Brother Saul'. He was willing to leave behind his anger and fear, and reach out to the person who threatened him most.

Saul was in dire need of Ananias' compassion. On his way to Damascus, he had had an extraordinary meeting with the Lord and been blinded during the encounter. He was wandering, confused, in that no-man's-land between conviction and conversion. Ananias was able to care for him and witness to him. As a result, Saul became a Christian. He was baptised and renamed Paul, and went on to become the greatest missionary the Church has ever known – all because Ananias cared for his enemy!

God-centred evangelism is about being willing to witness to those we find difficult, those who have wronged us, even those against whom we hold prejudices. Over the years, I have attended courses on racism awareness and seen people who had refused to admit they were racist finally being made aware of their prejudice. Our prejudices are often only camouflaged by a veneer of politeness. Jesus had the knack of seeing right through such veneers. He mixed with the outcasts of his generation and seemed to care most for the people society rejected. Wherever our prejudices lie, we should be aware that the Lord has a habit of sending to us just the kind of person we would really rather not see!

> Though I am free and belong to no man, I make myself a slave to everyone, to win as many as possible ... I have become all things to all men so that by all possible means I might save some.'
> 1 Corinthians 9:19,22

This statement was not an easy one for Paul to make. He was a Jew born of the tribe of Benjamin, trained by Gamaliel, a celebrated doctor of the Jewish law and, what was more, he was a Pharisee – one of the Jewish elite. He had everything going for him in the Jewish society from which he came. It was unthinkable for someone from such a social background to mix with people of other races, let alone love them and serve them like a slave! Yet Paul was willing to count his privileged background as nothing for the sake of serving Christ. He had to ditch his feelings of superiority and start getting alongside people where they were.

God-centred evangelism is about being available any time, anywhere and to anyone...

Full obedience to Christ leads to real effectiveness in witness. God-centred evangelism is about being available any time, anywhere and to anyone – taking the limits off our evangelism so that 'by all possible means we might save some'. There is a world of difference between the evangelist and the encyclopaedia salesperson, between the Christian who shares the eternal love of God and the insurance rep selling life policies. We are participating in God's work and its results can only fully be measured in eternity. If we are to be effective in evangelism, we must submit ourselves wholeheartedly to the love and will of our heavenly Father. If we are not wholly available, we cannot usefully participate in fulfilling the purposes of our Sovereign God; we haven't said, 'Any time, anywhere, anyone.'

4

PERSON-TO-PERSON EVANGELISM

When I was a student at university, I was very hard up financially. In sheer desperation, I applied for a job with an American company which promised high rewards to anyone who was confident, approachable and friendly. When I arrived for my first day at the new job, I discovered that it was selling encyclopaedias!

After an intensive and emotional four-hour training course, we were divided into teams and allocated prosperous suburban housing estates within a 30-mile radius of the regional office. As a 'trainee sales consultant', I followed a successful salesman from house to house and watched as he went through his well-rehearsed patter. It was fascinating. Within seconds of any door opening he had sized up the situation and tailored his pitch to match. Once he gained entry to a house, he generally found that he had a one-in-four chance of making the sale and charging in excess of a thousand pounds for a set of books.

I had three major misgivings about the technique – misgivings which became so disturbing that after three days I gave up the job. First, the salesman viewed each person as a target. They weren't people to him and he wasn't concerned about whether they needed what he was selling or, indeed, if they could really afford it. Second, he had a script which he recited. It was learnt by rote and therefore did not represent a true engagement with the people he was visiting. If at any point his 'client' tried to make him deviate from the script, he was quite unable to cope. Third, he had no time for people who didn't want to buy the product. At five points during his presentation he asked a question: a negative response to any of these meant that he was wasting his time and he would leave. As a committed Christian, I found this way of communicating with people unhealthy – particularly in that it made me look at others in a way that was unscrupulous and lacking in compassion. It was a very hard way to earn a living.

A few months later I went on a training course in personal evangelism hosted by an Anglican church near my hall of residence. During the day we were taught a kind of patter not dissimilar to that demonstrated by the encyclopaedia salesman. The same feelings of unease and disquiet returned. Over the years since then I have come across a number of similar evangelistic strategies which have claimed great results. Based on similar concepts to those employed by sects such as the Jehovah's Witnesses and Mormons – and by encyclopaedia salesmen – Christians are taught a 'patter'. During the course of door-to-door visits, they target potential converts and treat them like potential customers. This is not, to me, true evangelism; nor is it the kind of human relationship Jesus modelled.

> ... 'evangelism by rote' can do more harm than good.

I believe that 'evangelism by rote' can do more harm than good. If we treat people in this way, it can bring dishonour to the people of God and be a disservice to the work of the gospel. The most effective form of evangelism is friendship evangelism, which involves sharing the gospel within the context of real human relationships. Sadly, there are millions of Christians who do not have the know-how, the confidence or the experience to share their faith story in this way. There is a dormant army of evangelists waiting to be awoken for service in God's kingdom!

Some of us are naturally gifted in communicating, while others have to work very hard at it. Let's not forget, though, that non-verbal communication is as important as the words we speak. Experts tell us that generally words make up seven per cent, tone of voice 38 per cent and body language 55 per cent of the content of our communication. So, when people are listening to us, they are taking in much more than the words we are saying. Our posture, volume level, dress, speed of speech, appearance and attitude are all important too. Do we sound angry or patronising, for example? It doesn't matter how good our message is, if we have an off-putting manner or aren't sharing honestly from the reality of who we are, we can't be effective in personal evangelism.

If we look at the way Jesus spoke to people, and the value and respect he accorded each individual, we will begin to see how important this is. One example is his encounter with the Samaritan woman at the well. Jesus knew how to break the ice – he asked her for a drink. He asked open questions like, 'What do you want?' His conversation was full of interesting stories and illustrations. He showed her that he was interested in her as a person.

There are many different levels of human conversation. At the lowest level there is the 'How are you?' type of chat which may happen when you meet a colleague in the corridor or another parent at the school gate, for example. This is usually shallow and we don't really expect an honest answer. Then there's the 'Have you heard about?' level in which we shelter behind facts about others and bits of gossip. We give nothing away about ourselves and learn little about anyone else. The third level is, 'In my opinion...', when we begin to risk sharing something of our ideas, opinions and decisions. The moment the other person disagrees, we will probably retract and retreat to safer ground. Real communication is about more than having opinions and, at the fourth level, we begin to share our feelings and reveal something of our true selves. At the fifth and deepest level, we remove the mask and begin to trust others with the inner secrets of our lives as we open up to each other.

It is this fifth level, in my experience, which offers the best context for sharing the Christian message. Strangely enough, one can reach this level of conversation with another person either dreadfully slowly or surprisingly quickly. It can sometimes take years of regular contact with someone before a sufficient level of trust grows up, but I have sometimes known it happen in minutes!

I don't know what it is about trains, but they are often the best environment for moving along the relationship scale very quickly. Perhaps it is the anonymity of the journey and the fact that you are unlikely ever to meet each other again. I was once travelling alone on a near-empty train when an elderly man came down the corridor and asked if he could sit next to me. I was somewhat noncommittal because I was fairly tired and had relished the idea of some personal space. Within minutes he was telling me that he had been a Second World War bomber pilot, and that he was returning from the funeral of a lifelong friend who had been his co-pilot on many dangerous missions. We went quickly into a very deep level of sharing. Life, death, time, regret, forgiveness and God were all very much on the agenda. I had a God-given opportunity to share my faith, beginning where this man was at and with his questions about life after death. We were strangers on a train chatting intimately about life's journey.

Statistics show that very few people become Christians by just turning up at church and accepting the faith; for most, it is a slow process. We are living in a highly secularised society and we sometimes have to start off by just being 'shop windows' for the Lord long before others will want to know more.

A friend of mine, the vicar of a large church in central London, became a Christian during his stay with a Christian family overseas. They never spoke directly to him about Jesus, but he gradually became aware that Jesus lived in their home. It was by looking at their lives and experiencing the quality of their relationships that he was drawn to faith in Jesus himself.

John Finney's well-respected survey, *Finding Faith Today* (Bible Society, 1992), revealed that for 39 per cent of men and 40 per cent of women, a Christian friend was an important supportive factor in their coming to faith. For 15 per cent of men the main factor in their becoming Christians was the influence of a friend, and for women it was even higher, at 24 per cent. Christian friends are important, according to Finney's research, because they give 'love, understanding, care and prayers'.

When Jesus met him, Zacchaeus was not a popular man. He was considered a traitor because, as a tax collector, he was regarded as a Roman collaborator. Yet Jesus was willing to go to Zacchaeus' home and become his friend. Sometimes as Christians we can appear proud, judgemental and stand-offish to others. It is easy to categorise people in our dealings with them, to look on them as 'non-Christians' rather than 'not-yet-Christians'. However, our attitude should be about wanting to accompany them on the journey of faith rather than condemn them for not having any faith at all.

To many Christians, the big question about friendship evangelism is the most embarrassing: 'Have you got any non-Christian friends?' Some of the most frustrating experiences I have ever had as an evangelist stemmed from this problem. It would appear that there are churches around with congregations who have hardly any non-Christian friends. It is little wonder, then, that evangelism seems impossible! Where can they begin?

When someone becomes a Christian, they often want to leave their non-Christian friends behind and devote themselves to the life of their fellowship. That's so unfortunate, because their friendship network could be such a rich seam for personal evangelism. We must encourage new Christians to be witnesses for Jesus in the context of their ordinary life rather than leave it all behind for the sacred sanctuary of the fellowship!

Caring leads to listening

We have to earn the right to talk about Jesus, and one of the ways we can do this is by caring. It is because we care that people will listen. This aspect of mission is taught to our gap-year team members at the beginning of their orientation course with Share Jesus International. It is remarkable what stories they bring back with them months later. I recall one team describing how they discovered that a neighbour had lost her dog. They responded by showing the woman a deep sense of compassion and care during what was a very real time of crisis for her. They helped to prepare 'lost dog' posters to attach to lamp posts all over the area. They went out searching the neighbourhood with a photo of the dog. The dog was eventually found – and the woman's gratitude did more to advance evangelism on the estate than a thousand glossy handbills!

Another team began to hang around a local park, even buying skateboards to become part of the local 'teen scene'. They gained such skill in skateboarding, they earned street-cred and influence. One evening I visited them and was impressed to see a line of skateboards all the way up the garden path, while inside the skateboarders were having their weekly Bible study.

A third team noticed that local residents often had to queue for long periods before they could collect their pensions and benefits from the post office. They opened up the nearby church hall and served free tea and coffee, building bridges with people and opening the way for the Christian message.

> **If personal evangelism is to be effective, it must be set in the context of real, caring human relationships.**

When we knock on someone's door demanding a hearing, we have often not taken the time to care or the trouble to understand. If personal evangelism is to be effective, it must be set in the context of real, caring human relationships. When we care for the old man who is housebound, his neighbours will surely hear about it. When we care for the harassed young mum struggling to bring up a child alone, she will tell other mums at the school gate. When we care for the young people gathering in the park at night, their parents may well sigh with relief. Caring prepares the way for the gospel more effectively than the most dynamic mission programme. We must show that Christianity works *before* we try to persuade others of its credibility. And this caring is not just a preparation for evangelism; rather, it flows out of a deep sense of compassion for others given to us by the Lord.

Personal evangelism without caring can appear hard and heartless. Mission without compassion lacks the integrity and authenticity of the gospel. The most effective way of personal evangelism is to be someone's friend – and not just a fair weather friend, but a committed, caring and compassionate friend; someone who can be relied upon, come what may. Our great privilege is to introduce them to our Friend, who will accept them no matter where they've been, what they've done, how they've lived or who they are; a Friend who will begin a new life within them.

Every committed Christian should have an active concern for at least three or four non-Christian friends. When our mission teams go out, I ask them to produce a personal constituency – a sheet of paper listing the non-Christian people for whom they are praying and with whom they are sharing the gospel. It is fascinating to hear how names added to the list sometimes become friends, and out of those friendships come new disciples. I would encourage every Christian to maintain such a list. It provides a focus for personal evangelism and reminds us that we are all, in a sense, on mission all the time.

Some years ago a friend of mine was on a train travelling from Leeds to Birmingham. As he walked down the corridor, he prayed about where he should sit. He took a seat opposite a rather bored-looking woman. He began to talk to the woman about late-running trains, the weather and life in general. By the time the train reached Birmingham he had shared his testimony and taken out his Bible to look at some verses about Jesus with her. When the train arrived in Birmingham, however, he had to get off to attend a meeting. Frustrated that the conversation wasn't over, my friend gave the woman his Bible and wrote his address inside the cover in case she might like to write and ask him more.

Completely unknown to him, another Christian got on at Birmingham station and looked for somewhere to sit. As she walked down the carriage, she saw a woman reading a Bible, so she sat down opposite her. She began to ask her fellow passenger about her faith and soon discovered this woman's hunger to know more. By the time the train had arrived in Plymouth, the woman had found Jesus Christ and given her life to him. She wrote to my friend telling him what had happened. He was completely overwhelmed by the way God had used him.

Often it is when we move beyond our comfort zone and make

ourselves available to witness, to go on mission and to do evangelism, that our faith comes alive and we begin to live more fruitfully as disciples of Jesus Christ.

How to lead a person to Christ

I have sometimes been shocked to discover that people who have been Christians for many years, who take a leading role in the life of the church (even preaching and teaching), seem completely incapable of leading someone to faith. We never know when such an opportunity will present itself.

I was totally unprepared when on a British Airways flight to a conference in the Philippines I had an opportunity to tell someone about the gospel. It seems that the other twenty evangelists on board were in the same position, because when I asked if any of them had a Christian tract or gospel I could give away, not one of them had anything to hand!

I had noticed that the air hostess was looking tired and stressed. As she passed out the dinner trays, I looked up into her eyes and sensed a deep pain there. 'How are you?' I asked.

She paused, looking down at me. 'Are you really interested?' she said.

I nodded.

'Okay, I'll come and tell you after the dinner service is finished.'

She gave out all the meals, then came to sit over the aisle from me. She told me about how stressed she was, how lonely she felt and how tired she'd become. We began to talk and quickly we travelled up the scale to level five. I went with her to the galley and she made me a cup of coffee. As the conversation continued, she began to talk about her search for God. She explained that her flatmate had become a Christian and the transformation in her life had been so profound that she wanted to find Christ too. But she had never dared ask her friend exactly how it worked. A fellowship group had started to meet in the flat, but she had never been asked to go; so she had retreated to her room, just joining them for coffee at the end of each evening. The groundwork had been laid, the witness of her flatmate had borne fruit, and now she wanted to find Christ for herself.

As I had neither tract nor a spare Bible to hand, I used a little diagram to show how you become a Christian. She prayed with me there and then in the aircraft galley. Two weeks later I met her on the runway at Kuala Lumpa airport and gave her a Bible and some reading notes to get her started.

Having, perhaps, laboured the point that we should never approach personal evangelism as an opportunity to go through our Christian sales patter, I need to say that I do find it useful to have some kind of structure when I feel that someone is ready to hear and to respond. I'd have been lost without it in the aircraft galley that night!

Presenting the gospel

There are many possible ways of describing the process of salvation, and many clever diagrammatic methods have been devised, and I want to briefly outline the one I use. I certainly wouldn't want to use this as a formula for cold contact witnessing; neither would I stick rigidly to a script. I would simply sprinkle the key points about salvation through my conversation with the listener.

This nine-point outline I use in witnessing to non-Christians is an amalgam of several others, which I have adapted to a wide range of situations and listeners over the years. I'm sure there are other outlines which work equally well, but I commend it as a clear presentation of the process of salvation which can be easily understood by all kinds of different people.

1 A perfect world

There was a time when the world was perfect, and when God and people lived in perfect unity and understanding. God would never have made something that was imperfect. He looked at it and it was good! Creator and created were in relationship.

> In the beginning God created the heavens and the earth.
> *Genesis 1:1*

2 A fallen world

The perfection of the created order was stained, smashed and spoiled by humanity's rebellion. Because we were given free will, we had the option to reject God's way and go our own. Because of our selfishness, the world has been polluted by sin. What was perfect was made imperfect, and the special relationship that had existed between God and people was severed.

> 'For from within, out of men's hearts, come evil thoughts, sexual immorality, theft, murder, adultery, greed, malice, deceit, lewdness, envy, slander, arrogance and folly. All these evils come from inside and make a man unclean.'
> *Mark 7:21–23*

3 Sin separates

It's little wonder, then, that God seems far away. The rebellion and sinfulness of which we are a part, and the personal guilt which all of us carry, act as a barrier between us and God, like a cloud hiding the sun.

> But your iniquities have separated
>   you from your God;
> your sins have hidden his face from you,
>   so that he will not hear.
> *Isaiah 59:2*

4 All have sinned

Every one of us has to face up to our personal sin and failure. We are not only part of the fallen nature of the world around us, we have personally rejected God's ways by things we have said, thought and done. We may feel that we are 'good' or 'caring' or 'honest', but nevertheless we have failed in God's eyes. It's like in an examination where the pass mark is 50 per cent, and one candidate gets 5 per cent and another 49 per cent; both have still failed. The Bible teaches that every one of us, without exception, has failed to live up to God's standard.

> ...for all have sinned and fall short of the glory of God.
> *Romans 3:23*

5 Separation

This guilt and failure leads to our separation from a holy God. Nothing we could invent ourselves will bridge that gap. Philosophy, morality, good works and even religion are not enough to span the chasm between ourselves and our Maker. Even obedience to the Ten Commandments is not enough.

> Therefore, no one will be declared righteous in his sight by observing the law; rather, through the law we become conscious of sin.
> *Romans 3:20*

6 The cross

Every manmade solution to this problem of separation from God rests on our initiative, our works, our effort. Yet, that is all futile. Meanwhile, God has provided a way for us to know him and be one with him. This is not a reward for what we do. Instead, it comes by faith – and faith alone. It is when we recognise that we can't get to God on our own but need to put trust in him that we discover the way.

> Jesus answered, 'I am the way and the truth and the life. No one comes to the Father except through me. If you really knew me, you would know my Father as well.'
> *John 14:6,7*

7 Redemption

As we allow Jesus Christ to forgive us, change us and renew us, we become new people. We are 'born again' and discover the joy of this new relationship with God through Jesus Christ. As more and more people are redeemed, they affect the world and become part of the redemption of the world, which will be completed at the end of time.

> Therefore, if anyone is in Christ, he is a new creation; the old has gone, the new has come! All this is from God...
>
> *2 Corinthians 5:17,18*

8 Christian growth

When we have received Jesus Christ into our lives to save us and to redeem us, we begin a journey with him which is life-enriching and life-transforming. We grow as Christians by reading the Bible, praying, witnessing to and serving others, and through fellowship and worship:

❖ *Bible*:

> All Scripture is God-breathed and is useful for teaching, rebuking, correcting and training in righteousness, so that the man of God may be thoroughly equipped for every good work.
>
> *2 Timothy 3:16,17*

❖ *Prayer*:

> 'But when you pray, go into your room, close the door and pray to your Father, who is unseen. Then your Father, who sees what is done in secret, will reward you.'
>
> *Matthew 6:6*

❖ *Witness*:

> 'Therefore go and make disciples of all nations, baptising them in the name of the Father and of the Son and of the Holy Spirit.'
>
> *Matthew 28:19*

❖ *Worship*:

> 'Yet a time is coming and has now come when the true worshippers will worship the Father in spirit and truth, for they are the kind of

worshippers the Father seeks.'
John 4:23

9 Response

I find that many Christians are reticent about bringing to faith the people to whom they are witnessing. They often hesitate at the last hurdle, feeling unworthy or inadequate. Yet when we move to challenge someone directly about their response to Jesus, I believe the Holy Spirit comes to help us in a special way. Many times in my own witnessing I've been astonished how easy this last stage can be. When you ask, 'Would you like to become a Christian now?' the answer is regularly, 'Yes, please!' However, we can never make that response for another; they must do it themselves. It is a door only they can open. I never force a response, and if people want more time to consider their decision I always give it. If their conversion is to be genuine, it must be based on a wholehearted response, when they feel completely ready.

Ultimately, we can only lead people so far in their journey to Jesus. Logic, discussion and reason can take the enquirer a long way, but ultimately there must be faith – faith neither in me nor my religion, but faith in Jesus, the Saviour, the Way, the Truth and the Life.

'I stand at the door and knock. If anyone hears my voice and opens the door, I will come in and eat with him, and he with me.'
Revelation 3:20

A good starting point for personal evangelism is to attempt to discover the kind of God the other person believes or doesn't believe in. People like to talk about their beliefs and in a situation of trust and friendship I have found others more than willing to talk about their views on God.

Talking about Jesus

I started my own search for faith by venturing to find out more about the 'vague power' in the universe. As I began to question and debate,

I gradually discovered that the more I learned about Jesus, the more I discovered about God. I still vividly remember kneeling by myself in the woods of a youth camp outside Birmingham and asking Jesus Christ to come into my life. It took me a year of study, discussion and thought to move from my 'vague power' theory to the discovery that I could get to know this 'vague power' through the person of Jesus Christ.

We need to talk a lot about Jesus. The more we talk about him, the more people will want to know him. There is such a richness in his personality, they can't help but be intrigued by him. He is vulnerable, serious, funny, compassionate, thoughtful, serene, concerned, serving, humble, caring, rejected, suffering, anguished, broken... and so much more. When we begin to talk about Jesus, and to remind people that he is God's Son, we are setting before them the biblical view of God rather than the folk myths – in which God becomes the white-bearded old man, the policeman, the 'vague power' or the magician. We prepare the way for them to meet the true God, not the false gods of our secularised society. We are not trying to get them to put ticks by a set of concepts, like the encyclopaedia salesman. We are not inviting them to give assent to a doctrinal code, like those representing the sects. We are all about introducing people to a friend – Jesus Christ.

One of the darkest pastoral experiences of my whole ministry occurred just a few weeks after I took over my first church. I was summoned to a prison in Wakefield to hear a distraught man confess to murder. He had refused to speak to the police unless there was a 'priest' present, and his statement would be in the form of a confession. Having heard about me in the local newspaper, he chose me to be his 'priest'.

At my interview with him in the top security section of the prison, two murder squad detectives sat behind me taking notes. It was a bizarre and difficult experience. This intense moment of confession was the start of a friendship with this man which continued for years afterwards. He was torn apart by guilt and beside himself with regret. Gradually, however, as the months went by, I was able to talk to him about Jesus. The more he understood about Jesus, the more he began to recognise that Jesus could be a friend, even to him.

2

CHURCH-BASED
EVANGELISM

5

PRINCIPLES OF CHURCH-BASED EVANGELISM

The churches of the UK need to stop anticipating decline and start planning for growth. It is time they moved from maintenance to mission and put church-based evangelism at the top of the agenda.

The Church exists by mission in the same way that a fire exists by burning. It has been convincingly argued that mission is the hallmark of the genuine Church, and that the Great Commission – '… go and make disciples of all nations …' (Matthew 28:19) is the Church's most essential activity. Lesslie Newbigin, one of the most respected and influential theologians of the twentieth century, went further, suggesting that a Church which has lost its missionary vision is not an authentic New Testament Church. Evangelism is the Church's core task and the local church is the most appropriate place through which it should be done. Sadly, many churches have lost their vision for this work and don't commit any resources to doing it.

A hospital combines a number of functions. It is a hotel where people are housed; a restaurant where meals are served; a business office where records and accounts are kept. Above all else, however, a hospital is a place where people are healed; this is its essential activity. In the same way, the local church does many things – but its essential activity should be to lead people to Christ. All its other functions should always be secondary. Sadly, many churches don't seem to operate in this way.

Research projects in recent years have confirmed a diminishing commitment to the task of evangelism. Disturbing majorities of church leaders interviewed not only admitted that evangelism was not high on their agenda, but did not accept that the primary purpose of the Church was to share the good news of Jesus Christ. Most churches don't have an ongoing programme of evangelism, and many state that their congregation would be uncomfortable with such a programme.

I believe there is a huge resource of committed Christians waiting to be released into dynamic evangelistic outreach. We need to learn how to mobilise them, give them skills to reach the emerging generation, and show them how to use the local church as their base. If they are to be effective, they need to grasp the following basic principles of church-based evangelism.

Church-based evangelism must be incarnational

Some Christians commute several miles to church, park their cars and attend worship. Immediately after the service, they get back into their cars and drive several miles home again. Unfortunately, they have no midweek contact with the neighbourhood which forms the context for their church's mission. Churches consisting of commuter Christians like these can't do evangelism effectively. If a church is to be effective evangelistically, it must relate to the community in which it is set, and its congregation must constantly be building networks of relationship, service and witness within their locality. A church cut off from its community is like a tree cut off from its roots – weak and barren!

> **A church cut off from its community is like a tree cut off from its roots – weak and barren!**

Jesus' identification with humanity was complete. By his birth he 'became flesh and made his dwelling among us' (John 1:14); in his life he was 'numbered with the transgressors' (Isaiah 53:12); in his death he 'bore our sins in his body' (1 Peter 2:24). He 'shared in [our] humanity so that by his death he might destroy him who holds the power of death' (Hebrews 2:14). And he made his incarnation the model for the Church's mission. He told his disciples, 'As the Father has sent me, I am sending you' (John 20:21). The former bishop of Liverpool, David Sheppard, wrote (in *Bias to the Poor* published by Hodder & Stoughton): 'If we can believe God is really incarnate He is frighteningly close, and He meets us where we are. The followers of Jesus have to live in that world too: like Him we are called to meet people where they are.'

Church history is full of examples of Christians who have been willing to accept this painful model of incarnation as their method of mission. Throughout his ministry we see the apostle Paul becoming 'incarnate' within various communities. At Philippi he spoke with Lydia and other women by the riverbank; he shared a cell with prisoners in a jail. In Athens he debated with Jews and Greeks in the synagogue and the marketplace, and argued with Epicurean and Stoic philosophers. Paul's method of evangelism was all about meeting people where they were, relating to them in their own context and presenting the gospel in ways that were relevant to their felt needs and aspirations – incarnational evangelism at its best.

Another good example is the famous nineteenth-century missionary to China, Hudson Taylor. He adopted Chinese dress and customs and mingled freely with the Chinese people. It was a revolutionary style of working for his time. George Woodcock wrote in *The British in the Far East* (Weidenfeld & Nicolson, 1969):

> A belief in the equality of all men before God, too literally acted upon, can produce patterns of behaviour which no imperial society can accept with equanimity. To the Taipans and all the other people who believed that the white man's dignity rested in strict adherence to British dress and habits Hudson Taylor's action was deeply shocking. He had gone 'native'. He had lost face. He had broken the magic ring of white solidarity.

Just as Hudson Taylor needed to shed his cultural entrapment to become a living witness in Chinese society, so we as Christians must be willing to ditch much of our middle-class subculture if we are to become incarnate in contemporary society. However, this does not mean that we lose our identity. In becoming one of us, Jesus did not cease to be himself.

Church-based evangelism must reach the unreached

Many congregations who think they are 'doing evangelism' are in fact just talking to themselves. Their glossy handouts never get beyond the fringes of the fellowship, their guest services only bring in the 'lapsed', and their sermons only preach to the converted. It takes great commitment and determination for a church to 'reach the unreached'.

> **Evangelism to people who have never heard the true Christian message should be the highest priority for every church in the world.**

Evangelism to people who have never heard the true Christian message should be the highest priority for every church in the world. Sadly, many have turned their back on those who have never heard the good news. When scholar Rupert Davies examined the role of evangelism in the Methodist Church, he concluded (in *Testing of the Churches*, Epworth Press):

> It has, of course, not disowned the narrower and more intense forms of evangelism, but it has tended to leave them to certain vigorous groups within itself and often, too often, to evangelists from overseas.

Yet Methodism's founder, John Wesley, instructed his helpers to 'go always, not only to those who need you, but to those who need you most'. If we are to engage in effective evangelism, then we must be willing to move beyond the friendship networks of our fellowship and identify the 'unreached people groups' around us.

In traditional church life, it has been realised that we expect people first to behave, then to believe, then to belong. But Jesus did not adopt this approach in his ministry. He first welcomed people so that they belonged; then they could learn to behave, after which they believed.

> As Jesus went on from there, he saw a man named Matthew sitting at the tax collector's booth. 'Follow me,' he told him, and Matthew got up and followed him.
>
> *Mathew 9:9*

Matthew was first invited to belong; as he sat with the others disciples and heard Jesus' teaching, he learned what following Jesus was all about; then he believed. Personally, I am convinced that this is the right model for church evangelism. The first step is to encourage people to belong by accepting them into our community and inviting them to journey with us. As they become part of us, they learn what Christians believe and how to behave as citizens of God's kingdom. Then, as they see the difference faith is making in our lives, they can decide whether or not they want to share in our beliefs.

Church-based evangelism must be culturally relevant

Christians need to learn the language of those who cannot understand our religious terminology. Too often we are answering questions people are not asking, and speaking in ways that put them off. Sadly, many churches are so middle class in their language, dress, culture and thinking, they are unapproachable to those from working class or other backgrounds. As Clive Calver wrote in *The Truth about Truth* (Monarch, 1997):

> This is a class-ridden nation, and the Christian faith has become a middle class religion. In practice it often seems irrelevant to the working person. We need to free our faith from its cultural entrapment.

Those wanting to engage in church-based evangelism need to understand their target audience and how to communicate in ways they will hear and understand. A quarter of our population read neither newspapers nor books. The language of TV, film and music has become the vernacular of many, and is the language used by the contemporary media and modern advertising – communication which doesn't so much appeal to linear thinking as to 'gut reaction' and which uses images as much as words. Today, what you experience is as important as what you read – maybe more so. If the local church is offering forms of worship that are too cerebral and text-based, the message won't get through. Local church life and outreach must be seen to work and to be directly relevant to people's lives.

Church-based evangelism must be spiritual

The independent research charity The Tomorrow Project (www.tomorrowproject.net) claimed in 2006 that although Britain has more people identifying with non-Christian faiths than ever before and although the Church 'has moved to the edge of society': 'Interest in spirituality remains strong and may even have grown.'

The BBC Soul of Britain survey in 2000 showed that over 76 per cent of the population admitted to having had a spiritual experience such as answered prayer or a strong sense of God's presence. This was up by 59 per cent in just over ten years, and by more than 110 per cent in 25.

A couple of years ago, the *Sun* newspaper polled over 1000 adults on their beliefs. Among the results:

❖ 71 per cent believed in the existence of a soul.

❖ 70 per cent believed in a god or some form of higher power.

❖ 53 per cent believed in an afterlife.

❖ 44 per cent prayed once a week or more.

❖ 17 per cent said they had more faith in astrology and star signs than organised religion.

In late 2007, prayer hit the national headlines when the relief and development charity Tearfund announced the results of a new survey which claimed that 20 million people in the UK – a staggering 42 per cent – pray, with one in three adults believing that God watches over them. One in five believe prayer changes the world.

Meanwhile the biggest of the country's three exam boards reports a 21 per cent increase in the choice of Religious Studies at A-Level in the four years up to 2004. Numbers of students taking Philosophy A-Level have jumped by a staggering 67 per cent. Add to this the proliferation of prayer rooms or sacred spaces springing up in airports and other public places and the appointment of chaplains in the fields of commerce and industry and we have a picture of a highly secularised society that is seeking meaning and seems to maintain a residual understanding of Christian values.

So, increasingly, many are expressing a deep longing for love, for transcendence and identity. People are exploring new forms of popular spirituality. Thousands of ordinary people continue their inward journey of discovery in weekly yoga classes, t'ai chi groups, meditation sessions, aromatherapy clinics and occult covens in communities all over the country. The growth of interest in astrology, meditation and alternative medicine is offering a plethora of new religious perspectives.

This plurality of meaning is the driving force behind secularism and runs contrary to the Christian gospel. Twenty-first-century men and women 'pick and mix' their religious beliefs from a bewildering display in the supermarket of life.

A few years ago I crossed the threshold of a New Age shop in a small Devon town. I hoped none of my evangelical Christian friends would think I'd lost my senses as I browsed the bookshelves and eavesdropped on conversations. Customers in the shop – one of several similar stores in the high street – were buying books on meditation, tapes for relaxation, and homeopathic and health food products. Their search for spirituality had become part of the Saturday shopping ritual, sandwiched somewhere between Boots and Sainsbury's. The shop was busy. Spiritual things were being discussed freely, and there was an openness to anyone seeking a spiritual perspective on life. In fact, I wondered if there was more talk of the spiritual disciplines here than in the church directly opposite! All it advertised was an autumn bazaar and a holiday slide show.

Hunger for the spiritual has gone mainstream. I predict this trend will grow rapidly. The search for meaning is on. The eminent psychologist CJ Jung observed that among all his patients in the second half of their life (age 35 plus), there was not one whose problem was not that of lacking a religious outlook on life. We disregard the spiritual side of our existence at our peril. Sociologists tell us that the modern era ignored the spiritual dimension of our humanity in favour of scientific method; postmodernism, however, will reaffirm the importance of the mystical and the spiritual.

Those of us committed to evangelism must face up to the challenge of how we can start a meaningful dialogue with the world and demonstrate the power of the one true God for all to see. As the debate about explanation and meaning rolls ever onward, the question is: have we, as contemporary Christians, something meaningful to say to a world fascinated by religious questions but disinterested in traditional answers? How can we challenge the existentialist tolerance of different and relative truths: 'what is spiritual truth for you is true and what is spiritual truth for me is true, and I accept that your spiritual truth is as true as my own'? I find increasingly that people are not interested in talking about church, theology or doctrine. The question they are asking is, 'Does Christianity work for you?' We need to demonstrate that it really does and – what's more – that it can work for them as well.

Church-based evangelism must use preaching

The art of preaching is making a comeback. Not on church platforms or in cathedral pulpits, but in West End theatres, luxurious conference suites, five-star banqueting halls, city libraries and dark smoky bars. Thousands queue for tickets to hear Ben Elton, Billy Connolly or Jo Brand preach their various versions of the secular gospel – two-hour sermons, with ice creams in the interval. Corporate executives pay upwards of £100 a ticket to hear management gurus like Charles Handy expound their latest business theories spiced with humorous personal experiences. Retired politicians, pop stars, authors, newsreaders and sports personalities make a healthy living on the speaking circuit, delivering personal anecdotes over fine wine and gourmet food. In libraries and school halls up and down the UK, a new generation of public speakers is making a living by telling stories. The growth of the comedy-club circuit has been astronomic in recent years, giving a wonderful new opportunity for radical young comedians to rehearse 40-minute routines based largely on anecdotal stories. Believe it or not, preaching (that is, one person talking to a lot of other people) is popular once again.

As usual, local churches are the last to catch on! We are still in 'Can you keep it short, please, pastor?' mode. Everywhere I go, I hear that church leaders are lengthening the worship, replacing the sermon with 'discussion groups', filling the church with fancy visual aids and suggesting that preaching is inappropriate for a television culture.

There is a feeling in many churches that the era of evangelistic preaching is dead – inappropriate to our culture and incongruous for our time. But it's time we recognised that the evangelistic sermon is one of the most compelling means of communication known. History should remind us that God speaks through the preached word and the human heart on fire for him. I personally believe that preaching *is* a relevant method of com-

... the evangelistic sermon is one of the most compelling means of communication known.

munication and the Church should rescue it from the ecclesiastical rubbish heap before it's too late! A good preacher's life experiences and personality are the greatest visual aids we can ever use. They will always be relevant because a preacher who has been listening to her audience carefully is actually engaging in a conversation with them; it's just her turn to speak.

Recently, I was at a conference of around seventy young preachers. They were from diverse denominational backgrounds and many of them were in their twenties. I heard their pain, sensed their frustration, saw the wasted opportunity of gifts unused. Many of them have never been affirmed by their pastor, never been given an opportunity to test their call, never had helpful sermon critique let alone been given basic skills in the craft of evangelistic sermon-making. Many church leaders have chosen to 'go with the flow', letting the worship speak and getting trendy with big-screen video and sound-bite messages. In so doing they have lost the greatest means of communication God ever gave to the Church – the preacher! We have gagged the emerging generation of evangelistic preachers whom God has called for us. The gospel messages God is giving them go unheard, and the anointing he has poured out on them is going down the drain.

For more than a generation, the evangelistic preacher has had a bad deal. He has been mocked by the media, misunderstood by the world and marginalised by the Church. There are endless courses, conferences and consultations on the role of the worship leader, but evangelistic preaching remains the Cinderella ministry of the contemporary church. I personally believe that it's time for evangelistic preaching to make a comeback!

Church-based evangelism must understand gender issues

A few years ago I was given two press tickets to a lecture. I wouldn't normally want to spend the whole of a Friday evening at a lecture, but this was quite an event! It was a two-and-a-half hour 'sermon' delivered by John Gray, author of one of the most popular books on the planet: *Men Are from Mars, Women Are from Venus.*

Several hundred well-dressed professionals crowded into the theatre, each having paid between £25 and £45 per ticket, while my wife and I were ushered into a private bar to meet Mr Gray and to mingle with the media glitterati.

Throughout his lecture, Gray talked in spiritual terms. Some of the spiritual language he used would be recognisable in any church setting. Yet I felt uneasy. At the end of the presentation I plucked up the courage to ask Gray's press agent directly, 'Is this spirituality he's advocating Christian?' The tall gentleman beamed at me. 'No way,' he said. 'John gets his inspiration from the East.' He went on to explain that John would be giving more attention to Eastern meditation techniques in his next seminar, which would be entitled, 'How to get what you want.'

So this popular guru is not a Christian, and his teaching stems from a philosophy vastly different to that of Jesus Christ. It's a religion of self-help rather than God-help. And there's a lot of common sense in what he teaches.

Gray's mission is to help individuals recognise that their partner comes from a 'different planet'. Once this has been appreciated, they can relax and cooperate with the differences instead of resisting or trying to change them. He points out that, for example, most women like to talk about their day, while most men don't. Women like to watch TV programmes in their entirety; men prefer to surf with the remote control. Tidiness is important to a woman; it's not so crucial for a man. Younger men are sexually aroused quickly; women more slowly. Men like to solve problems while women prefer to discuss them. Women don't like to ask men for emotional support; men don't offer it instinctively – they like to be asked!

Gray's organisation works with corporations and industries in facilitating a greater understanding between the sexes at work. By helping men and women work through their differences, the claim is that there is improved teamwork, efficiency and communication.

After years of counselling people with relationship problems, Gray has evidently stumbled on some very practical advice. It is clear to anyone who mixes with the opposite sex that men are very different from women. Whether this is biological or cultural is irrelevant; we know that these differences exist. Local church-based evangelism must begin to address the fact that women think, relate and make decisions in very different ways from men.

I personally advocate some all-male and all-female meetings as part of local church-based evangelism. I'm convinced that we need to learn how to present the gospel to men and women in different ways and how to take gender into account. 'Colour me Beautiful' programmes for women, for example, have been effective and popular. An expert in skin tone and fashion lectured over a hundred suburban women at a local church mission I was leading near Sheffield, demonstrating the importance of colour coordination, poise and style. Her excellent talk led to a personal testimony about inner wholeness which spoke of Christ's transforming power in her own life. Meanwhile, a group of men were meeting in a local pub to discuss stress at work. A trained leader helped them to identify the pressures they were facing and taught how prayer and Christian meditation could help.

Much work needs to be done on issues of gender in evangelism. We must learn much more about how men and women think, respond and make decisions if we want to be truly effective. What better way is there to ensure that this is done than by having male and female evangelists on every team! Sadly, many churches see the role of evangelist as exclusively male. I would like to see more women called to and affirmed in this work. One thing is for sure: one of the most effective evangelists Jesus encountered during his ministry was the woman from Samaria: many people from her town came to believe because of her testimony!

Church-based evangelism must be sensitive to personality

There are all sorts of theories around today for defining personality types. One of the most popular, the Myers-Briggs Type Indicator, was developed by Katherine Briggs and her daughter. Briggs was fascinated by the similarities and differences between people and began to develop lists of characteristics. Just after the Second World War she discovered that psychologist Carl Jung had developed a similar system, so she began to adapt his 'theory of types'.

Jung's primary distinction was between extrovert and introvert types. He suggested that extroverts prefer to focus on the outer world of things and people, and draw their energy from there. Introverts, however, prefer to focus on the inner world of ideas and concepts, and draw energy from there. This kind of analysis makes a lot of sense. We all know people who are more bubbly and outgoing and some who are more quiet and reserved. This, however, is only the beginning of the Myers-Briggs Indicator!

I went on a three-day Myers-Briggs course and found it challenging. Through lectures and questionnaires, the tutor led ten of us intrepid personality explorers through two ways of perceiving, (sensing and judging), two ways of making decisions (thinking and feeling), and two ways of living (judging and perceiving), until most of us in the group could clearly see which 'type' most described us. I sighed with relief as I began to discover myself clearly described in the descriptions of my personality type. It made me recognise where my weaknesses are, and why I have chosen so many people who are better at organising minutiae, making decisions and being logical to work in my team. They are there to complement me in my weaknesses!

As the course continued, however, I began to realise that these theories have an important application in the evangelistic outreach of the Church. Who do many churches appoint to welcome newcomers at the door, for example? The most extrovert member of the congregation! But what does that do to an introvert attending church for the first time? It frightens them away for ever! An introvert would much prefer no welcome at all, but a noticeboard, some personal space and the opportunity to meet people in a non-threatening way at their own pace.

I then began to reflect on the different styles of church evangelism I have engaged in over the years, and how some of them must have been deeply threatening to people of certain personality types. As someone who has been a travelling evangelist for nearly twenty years, I can see clearly that much of the evangelism I have engaged in has probably appealed more to extroverts like myself, with little effective evangelism among introverts.

Myers-Briggs is only a theory, and pushed to the limit I'm pretty sure it's a theory that might break down. It does, however, remind all of us in church life of one very important fact: people are different. If we use the wrong styles of evangelism on the wrong people, we may alienate or even damage them. A football stadium and an opportunity to step out publicly in front of 50,000 onlookers may appeal to some – but will scare the living daylights out of others. A friendly Alpha group that meets the needs of some might be a hellish ordeal for others. We need to learn how to get alongside different people in different ways just as Jesus did. One thing's for sure, however: he is calling us all to follow him, no matter what personality type we may have.

6

PREPARATIONS FOR LOCAL CHURCH EVANGELISM

I n chapter one I described one of the first missions I ever led, at the beach resort of Newquay in Cornwall. It was great fun! Every day scores of children and young teenagers gathered on the beach for stories and games, and we really enjoyed getting to know them.

As the days went by, some of these kids wanted to know more about Jesus, and members of our team had the privilege of leading several to Christ. We were overjoyed – but soon realised we had no effective way of following them up. Within a couple of days they would return home and our team would be dispersed throughout the country. We began to phone round our contacts in the area where these young people lived. However, it became clear how difficult it was to introduce a stranger to a church they knew nothing about and where nobody knew them.

There was an enormous sense of frustration at not being able to follow up these young converts, but through it I learned an important lesson: the best base for evangelism is not a holiday beach but a local church. The most effective team for witness and follow up in a community isn't a disparate team who are here today and gone tomorrow, but a group of local Christians who live their lives as though they are always 'on mission'.

In many towns and cities, God's greatest tool for evangelism – the local church – has become a blunt instrument. Congregations don't recognise the crucial importance of this outreach ministry and follow an agenda which is more about servicing the flock than searching for lost sheep. Here and there I am encouraged to see that some churches are waking up to the task and rediscovering the vital role they can play in the evangelisation of their area. If every local church was functioning evangelistically, there would be a natural link between its ongoing witness in the community, its outreach through sharing the faith, and its nurture of new Christians. Every church should function like a mission team! The local church is the God-ordained unit for mission and it's time that each fellowship developed a sense of responsibility for evangelism in their area. The motivation shouldn't be to 'get extra members' but to fulfil Christ's commission to 'go into all the world and preach the gospel'.

For more than twenty years, Share Jesus teams in different parts of the world have worked with hundreds of churches to help them evangelise their neighbourhoods. Although the actual mission may take only a week, the work of preparation for the mission begins months beforehand. Time after time, local ministers say that this process of preparation has been invaluable. Many churches actually rediscover their evangelistic ministry long before the week of mission begins.

The seven processes we facilitate in the run-up to a Share Jesus mission are listed below. My hope is that they may be adapted and modified for local situations in any part of the world!

1 Praying for the church

Some years ago a Korean minister arrived at our church in Raynes Park, London, and asked if he could rent a room. Our premises are fairly well used but when he explained that he needed the room from five until eight in the morning there didn't seem to be much of a problem!

Arriving at my office a few days later, I stopped in amazement. Echoing down the stairwell was the voice of this stranger, crying out to God in the Korean language for our church and for the people of Raynes Park. As I got to know him better, he explained that there could be no revival without prayer. He believed that prayer is the key to fruitfulness in the kingdom of God. I felt humbled and convicted by this stranger's commitment to pray for a neighbourhood and a church so far from his home.

I'm convinced that church mission without commitment to prayer is largely a waste of time. Prayer is the single most important factor in moving a church to mission. I know that when I pray for my own church and community, something significant happens in me! I begin to view the whole concept of mission in a different way. When I prayer-walked the streets near my home, I began to sense the spiritual needs of those who lived around me as never before. When I prayed with a small group of friends for my neighbours, I focused on their need for Christ as never before. When I joined with a local congregation to cry out to God for the needs of our area deep into the night, I sensed his blessing in special ways.

> **Prayer is the fuel for mission. When prayer dries up, mission usually splutters to a halt.**

Prayer is the fuel for mission. When prayer dries up, mission usually splutters to a halt. Those engaging in mission must be reliant on prayer, and they must see prayer as the key to their effectiveness. Something significant happens in the fellowship when people pray: God begins to work in significant ways.

2 Believing in growth

When a church is in decline, it can be demoralising for everyone involved. For many years I only ever seemed to attend church meetings in which decline and retrenchment were featured. The conversation centred on such questions as, 'Shall we close this church? Withdraw the minister? Stop the work?' This kind of defensive thinking can have a deeply disturbing effect on church life. Many congregations don't seem to believe that it's possible for their church to grow. Some find it incredible that people can come to faith in Jesus in the twenty-first century! However, there are many books and resources on church growth, and I would encourage church leaders to study them. While many struggle with any kind of formula for growth, I am sure there are principles we can all learn and understand.

Strategists tell us that there are a variety of ways in which a church can grow. First, there is internal growth in which Christians within a church become better disciples. This is essentially growth in quality rather than quantity, but it may mean that some people within the life of the church become committed Christians. We must never forget to evangelise within the church as well as outside it!

Then there is the kind of growth that involves expansion, when a church decides to get out among the unchurched in its community and win them for Christ; these new disciples are then nurtured in the context of the local church. Many missions and guest services work on this principle and it continues to be very effective. Every church should be doing it as part of its ongoing programme of activities.

Then there is the growth that happens when a church identifies a specific group of people who have no Christian witness among them. Reaching such a group will probably mean that church members will have to go to live and work among them. Through being present, through their service and witness, it's likely that some local people will become Christians and be linked with the fellowship. This kind of mission is generally considered to be the most effective evangelistic method of all. Many of Britain's most successful house churches have used this model extensively.

Finally, but most difficult of all, there's the growth that occurs when a church seeks to start a new church in a different culture to its own. This will involve pioneer church planters becoming completely at home culturally in a different community.

If we are to prepare a local church for mission, then we must create a faith context in which men and women believe that their church can grow, asking God for growth and expecting growth to happen. Without this theological and spiritual base, all mission will seem like a set of programmes rather than a strategy for helping the church to grow. The aim is to create an atmosphere in which there is a continuous drive towards growth.

3 Asking painful questions

As part of the move to encourage prayer and build faith, church leaders might find it helpful to undertake a comprehensive survey of their church's life and ministry. This isn't easy, and it's important that everyone takes part and looks at the process positively and constructively.

Counting the flock

Gibbs, Pointer and McGavran – three of the world's leading church growth experts – all agree that churches should regularly count their attendees, community roll and membership, to ascertain where there is decline and where there is growth. These experts believe that detailed surveys of churches should be undertaken to check their spiritual health. McGavran uses the example of a nurse using a thermometer to assess the patient's temperature; the thermometer will not help the patient to get better but it is a tool to help diagnose his or her condition. In the same way, church growth surveys don't help the church to grow, but they give an assessment of the church's health so that an intelligent diagnosis can be made.

Defending the activity of counting people, McGavran argues that because the church is made up of countable people, there is nothing particularly spiritual in not counting them. The numerical approach is used in all kinds of human endeavour, including industry, commerce, finance, research, government and invention; much of human enterprise is developed by continual measurement.

As trends of growth and decline in the local church are identified and tabulated, the information can be studied and discussed by everyone involved to determine what has been happening in the life of their church.

Plotting where people live

The next task is to plot the location of the church membership on a large map of the area. At Share Jesus we do this with many of the churches we work with, and the results are often startling. It is surprising how many churches have never undertaken such a simple exercise. Time and again, when I've done this simple exercise with church groups, we have discovered that members live in one area of town or in clusters around the neighbourhood – but quite often don't live near the church. Indeed, I've worked with some churches which have hardly any members living in their immediate catchment area at all!

When I begin to ask questions about these clusters, I sometimes discover that the members all come from one social group. I came across a startling example of this in a small town in Bedfordshire. When the leaders plotted their church membership, they discovered that every one of them lived on the chapel side of a main road. This was the old village community, which tended to be more middle class. There wasn't a single member living on the large council overspill estate on the other side of the road. The main road marked a gulf between two communities and the folk on the other side of the road were an unreached people group as far as the church was concerned. This church's mission audit led them to recognise their own exclusiveness, their lack of witness among a needy group of people living close by, and their ineffectiveness in reaching the young people in their neighbourhood. It led to the planting of a new work across the road, beginning in the school and the workingmen's club, and leading to evangelistic groups meeting in various homes.

Part of a church mission audit is to identify people groups, blocks of housing, streets or neighbourhoods where there is little or no Christian witness. These could well be rich seams for the gospel if there is effective evangelism among them.

Telling the church's story

Every church has a history – a history of success and failure, growth and decline, good times and bad. If a church is to engage in effective mission, it is important that this story is told. Our mission teams have developed a questionnaire on this, for use in local churches, and this is used as a trigger for discussion. (It is included in Appendix 1 at the end of this book.) We often find that as church members fill in the questionnaire, the discussion it generates is valuable as an exercise in itself. It enables people to talk about their church, to review the groups within it and the church's life generally. They can also explore the church's relationship to the community. When a church begins to ask fundamental questions like 'What are we trying to do?', 'How effective are we?' and 'Where are we heading?' this provides a natural forum in which mission and evangelism can be discussed and initiated. The questionnaire is designed to enable church members to face facts and get real with each other. It will not facilitate mission if we live in a kind of sanctified escapism in which hard questions are not faced and difficult decisions not made.

Looking inward, looking outward

The next task is to assess a church's effectiveness in evangelism. One of the quickest ways of doing this is to ask the various groups in the church – from the women's fellowship to the Boys' Brigade, from the mother and toddler group to the midweek Bible study – to undertake a period of self-assessment, looking at the way in which they welcome newcomers. When our mission teams undertake this work in a local church, we often invite each organisation to score its effectiveness as an agent for outreach in the church's life, and then to look at its pattern of growth or decline over recent years. Their leaders are invited to help them make this assessment by asking searching questions. Who has joined? Why have they joined? How has their belonging helped them in their pilgrimage of faith?

The responses to these questions must be handled compassionately and with care. There should be no sense of competition or comparison between different groups but rather an attempt by all of them to identify ways of developing their effectiveness in evangelism. Those that take the findings seriously are sometimes disturbed or even devastated by the results of these surveys. I have known some completely revamp their programmes so that they have a greater interface with the local community or a more prominent evangelistic emphasis.

Preparing a report

Collating all this information should give church leaders a broad idea of their congregation's effectiveness in mission. Findings about the church's strengths and weaknesses need to be thought through and addressed. It is sometimes helpful to bring in an outside consultant to help leaders articulate the story to the congregation. They may be too close to what's happening to unpack it creatively and look at it in the cold light of reason. The story may be about growth, decline, secession, division, failure, success, tradition, institution or pain. Telling this story can be therapeutic in itself and healing can result if the process is handled well. Sometimes churches can't move on in mission until they have resolved aspects of their history which hold them back.

Growing dissatisfied!

Church mission audits can facilitate evangelism by creating a holy unease which jump-starts a membership out of despondency or complacency, helping them see decline as unacceptable and moving them on to begin local outreach. Business executives of the world's most successful corporations are taught this restless dissatisfaction as a management tool. It is a healthy state of mind which drives the company forward to become more efficient and identify new markets. When I read the book of Acts I sense a similar hunger for growth.

So the process of auditing should create a feeling of dissatisfaction with who we are, what we do and how we function. This dissatisfaction is the key to mobilising a church for mission and evangelism. Where a church fellowship remains smug and self-satisfied, it won't see the need for evangelism or glimpse a vision for the world.

Another benefit of an audit is that it can sometimes prompt churches to work more closely with other groups of Christians in their area. I am sure that where churches work together in mission, God blesses in special ways. Different fellowships have different gifts and strengths, and they may be more effective in winning men and women for Christ if they work in partnership.

Remember that completing an audit is a tool that can give you a basis for evangelism or paint a picture that helps you imagine mission. But don't get caught up in the detail of interpreting the findings;

the relational aspect of sharing Jesus is the most important thing and the audit is just one way to facilitate that.

If you prefer not to use or adapt some of the questions for audit supplied in the appendices, you could borrow the SMART approach from the world of business. Use the acronym to help you define your mission goals:

S – specific (or significant or stretching)
M – measurable (or meaningful or motivational)
A – achievable (or attainable)
R – realistic (or relevant, or reasonable)
T – timely (or trackable)

4 Understanding your community

Having audited the life of the local congregation, the next step is to look at the context in which the church is set and to assess how best to do evangelism within it.

When missionaries go to other countries they often spend months looking at the cultural, sociological, religious and economic profiles of the group they will be working with. Rarely, if ever, do local church congregations undertake a similar discipline when looking at the context for their evangelism! It's little wonder, then, that we are often saying the wrong things at the wrong time to the wrong people. A few hours of research in the local library or among the housing and employment statistics in the local council records office can be very revealing. It is sometimes even possible to purchase a demographic and socio-economic survey of an area from the local council.

One of the best ways to engage a congregation in confronting the needs and possibilities of its catchment area is to get them to do the survey. There are a wide range of basic formats for doing this on offer from different mission agencies. The one we use in Share Jesus seeks to gain a deeper understanding of the nature of the local community, its strengths, weaknesses and friendliness. (A sample is included in Appendix 2.) In conducting the survey, we generally train our interviewers to introduce themselves as coming from the local church which is trying to discover ways of serving their community more effectively. When church members carry out this survey, they begin to understand better the felt needs of people in the neighbourhood instead of relying on their own, often outdated, assumptions. The aim is not to provide opportunities for personal evangelism, but to give Christians a feel for the mission field around them

Some years ago I was working with a congregation which was deeply concerned about its lack of children's outreach. Years before the church had been well known for its Sunday school, which had numbered hundreds of attendees. When they completed their community survey they discovered, to their amazement, that there were hardly any children living in the area! The population had aged, children had grown up and moved away; even the local school was threatened with closure. Their research helped them to recognise that children's work was inappropriate for their context. Instead they invested time and energy in developing effective programmes of outreach for the elderly and the housebound. A similar survey carried out ten years later might well reveal that the estate was filling up with young couples and the area repopulating with children again! Community surveys, then, are not a once in a lifetime activity for a church: they should be done again and again over time.

The community survey helps identify who is living around the church. Also, more importantly, it shows how people feel about the area and what they are looking for. When the congregation bridges the gap between what they think people need and what people actually want, the church will become more effective in mission and evangelism.

5 Welcoming the world!

In the village life of previous centuries the whole community network seemed to revolve around church, pub and shop. You could look at the geographical parish in which the church was set and seek ways of reaching that defined area and population for Christ.

Today the huge urbanised areas which make up the UK are vastly different. Where I live in south-west London it is hard to find any geographical boundaries between the different boroughs. Sociologists tell us that people who live in large cities do not have a geographical view of the community in which they live. Their relationships are based around places of work, leisure, the school, the club, the pub, the hobby or sporting group and the learning centre. Evangelism in this context should be less about trying to reach the entire population of a geographical area and more about witnessing to the different people groups. In the words of Peter Anthony in *Managing Culture* (Open University Press, 1994):

> [C]ultures develop in communities which are distinctive from their neighbours and are held together by patterns of economic and social cooperation reinforced by custom, language, tradition, history and networks of moral interdependence and reciprocity. As these are established and sedimented over time they lead to customary understandings and obligations, patterns of expectations that do not require to be calculated or defended.

Churches need to witness within these cultures and absorb their characteristics if they are to be relevant and welcoming. Does the church have little or no contact with young couples, for example? Are there too few men in the congregation? What about ethnic minorities? Teens? Divorced or separated people? Are working-class people poorly represented compared with the local sociological profile?

One of the best ways to reach a people group is to develop personal relationships with the people in them and then to form a small home-based cell group – sometimes called a kinship or neighbourhood group. This cell group is basically a church, and Christian conversion happens as non-Christians join the group and gradually accept the message of Jesus. They, in turn, invite their friends to join them in forming another group. In this way the church self-perpetuates, forming a new cell group with each cycle. Such small groups help bring about the contextualisation of the church as it becomes focused on different cultural groups – young people, single parents, the over-sixties, people from a specific ethnic group, or those from a working-class or middle-class background. Nevertheless, it is important that such groups relate to one another and to the mother church to foster a rich diversity of membership.

The church of the twenty-first century will be the church of many small groups. Some of these may meet on church premises and be drawn from different ethnic or socio-economic backgrounds. Others may meet in a tightly zoned geographic area, where two or three couples of the same socio-economic background meet together and form their own neighbourhood cell. Some groups may share a specific interest, background, workplace or experience; others may consist of, for example, ex-offenders, unemployed young people, executives, housewives or singles.

> **The church of the 21st century will be the church of many small groups.**

In Share Jesus we ask local church leaders to identify at least ten people groups in their area, and to make initial contact with them. Churches which do this, using mission teams to help them, have the most effective mission experiences. Recently I came across a list of people groups which one of our host churches identified on a rough estate in Glasgow. They found that there were identifiable groups of single parents, bingo fans, workingmen's club members, street kids, elderly housebound, alcoholics and drug users. Their strategy for mission was based not around reaching the area, but around getting alongside these groups, winning their confidence, meeting their needs and witnessing in real-life situations.

From the information gleaned in the community survey, then, it should be possible to identify groups of people in your community who are unreached and in need of the Saviour. This is important information in devising a strategy for a local church to grow.

6 Developing aims and goals

Using these techniques, helps church leaders identify realistic and achievable goals for their local mission. These should be prioritised and ways identified in which they might be accomplished.

It is vital that there is joint ownership of these goals by the whole congregation. Attaining them will be costly in terms of energy, finance and commitment, and it is crucial that there is broad agreement on what the priorities are. There should probably only be about two or three in total and, most importantly, they should be achievable! Some examples of aims and goals identified by churches working with us at Share Jesus include:

❖ *Deepening spiritual life* – renewing the devotional life of the church corporately and individually; drawing the membership together into closer fellowship; seeking fresh vision and hope for the future.

❖ *Proclaiming Jesus within the local community* – highlighting the profile of the local church within the community; breaking down the culture gap between church and society; making practical links of friendship with the local community; seeking to bring people into a living relationship with Jesus Christ.

❖ *Outreach among teens* – encouraging the development of youth work within the church, if necessary beginning new groups; making contact with teens outside the Church; seeking to lead them to Christ; beginning some kind of initial contact with detached young people in the community

❖ *Mission among children* – engaging in mission among children, seeking to strengthen existing children's work; telling the Jesus story in imaginative and exciting ways to children in the neighbourhood.

There are as many different aims and goals as there are churches. Others examples are identified in Appendix 4.

7 Writing a vision statement

If you were involved in running a business or corporation, you would be foolish indeed if you did not engage in strategic management.

The world is changing; society is changing; people are changing. And this rate of change is accelerating! Any business wanting to survive must be aware of this and constantly adjusting itself. Good businesses do not react to change after it has happened; they are actively predicting change and responding to it before it occurs. If a church is to be effective in evangelism, it needs to be regularly reviewing its life in the light of the changing mission context in which it is set.

When I took part in a management conference for entrepreneurial business people in Sheffield, I discovered that most fast-growing companies have a vision statement – a declaration of where the organisation is headed in the next five or ten years. It has been encouraging to see that many churches around the UK have been adopting mission statements in recent years, as they seek to define what they are trying to do and how they are trying to do it. Very few churches, however, have yet identified the strategic importance of a vision statement (see Appendix 3). This plans the future course, charts the way ahead and sets goals for growth for the coming years. Little wonder, then, that many churches have no real plan for growth. They are too busy with now to think about tomorrow. But churches which don't anticipate growth or plan for new life are unlikely to achieve them.

Anyone who has taken a course in contemporary management will know of the popular writings of Charles Handy. His concept of the 'Sigmoid Curve' is very relevant to many churches today. Handy suggests that every organisation, institution, group or team comes to a point where it peaks in its effectiveness and performance. Only by constant appraisal can the organisation identify the flattening out of its performance; and when this happens it must develop a new initiative, a new challenge, a new entrepreneurial vision, a new means of serving the market, and build towards another peak. If it fails to do this, it will surely decline.

As a church tries to formulate its vision, the congregation must be consulted so that they take ownership of the aims and goals identified. If local people understand the importance of these aims and goals, they are more likely to get involved and to feel included as the mission strategy develops. Every goal should be thought of as a 'faith target' and as such should be affirmed and celebrated.

As these aims and goals are drawn together into a statement the whole church owns, shared vision should shape the direction of the church's mission and all its ongoing objectives. I believe that the whole process will encourage the church to look at the bigger picture and see beyond the immediacy of their need for a new boiler or a better signboard! It can develop a sense of hope, which is a gift of the Holy Spirit. It is this visionary hope which looks to Jesus as the Lord of the harvest, and which recognises that his commission to 'go into all the world' is just as relevant to churches as to individuals. This is not the end but the beginning. It is the start of a new determination by the congregation to move out from behind the walls of church life and into effective mission in the world.

7

PLANNING A LOCAL CHURCH-BASED MISSION

In 1984 I took about sixty people on a mission based in churches around North London. We called the project Share Jesus to remind us that, whatever else we did, our most important task was to introduce Jesus to others. Since then Share Jesus has grown dramatically. Every year hundreds of Christians in the UK join Share Jesus teams on a week-long project and about the same number engage in similar missions across the US through the sister organisation Celebrate Jesus (www.cjmission.org).

I've discovered that the best evangelists are not necessarily ministers or church leaders, but ordinary Christian men and women. To be effective in evangelism, you don't need a degree in theology or a three-year course on mission. When ordinary people launch out into mission, God anoints them and uses them in a special way. I believe this is because he sees his people becoming dependent upon him. They recognise that they can't do this work in their own strength, and they want to work in partnership with him.

Christians who have never been on mission or who belong to a church which is not mission-minded are missing out! When ordinary Christians move out to witness in parks, pubs, schools and streets, they move out of their comfort zone. The work of mission brings us to a place of personal inadequacy and weakness where we have to rely on God's guidance for the right words to say and the right things to do. This place of vulnerability is the best place for Christians to be. The model is transformed as we adapt it to local situations; for example, in Cornwall Share Jesus teams are involved in Dawn Patrol

(God on the Beach) using lay people in mission.

All four Gospels end with Jesus Christ instructing his disciples to evangelise. The best known reference is in Matthew 28:18–20, often called 'the Great Commission':

> 'All authority in heaven and on earth has been given to me. Therefore go and make disciples of all nations, baptising them in the name of the Father and of the Son and of the Holy Spirit, and teaching them to obey everything I have commanded you. And surely I am with you always, to the very end of the age.'

The Christian faith is a faith to give away. The Scriptures constantly encourage us to share our faith in Christ. The most important motivation for evangelism is the love of God. The gospel is not to be shared in a pushy way but in a style that demonstrates God's love.

What is a mission?

When I first began to talk about mission to ministers in 1984, I didn't find much enthusiasm. Their mental image was usually of a week-long programme of evening rallies, with busloads of other Christians coming in to hear the big name preacher, a huge choir and all the trappings of what people call a crusade. Many were very antagonistic to this format for mission, saying that they had tried it but it didn't work, that it was 'blatant emotional manipulation' or just plain 'old-fashioned'. The general view was that such endeavours produced little lasting fruit and were followed by a huge feeling of anti-climax in the local church. I had to make it clear again and again that what they thought of as mission and what I was proposing were two very different things! Even so, some couldn't be persuaded to give our Share Jesus style of evangelism a try.

I have been fighting this kind of prejudice ever since. Much of my work over 25 years as a national and international evangelist has been about persuading church leaders to take a fresh look at the potential of local, church-based mission. It has often been an uphill task trying to introduce them to new models of evangelism which are about empowering Christians to Share Jesus in their neighbourhoods, and to persuade them that traditional models which aim to 'bring the community to the church' are dead. In a highly secularised society, church-based mission must be about bridging the gap between church and community, about building real relationships with local people and about Christians sharing their faith with people where they are. It is about taking the church out into the world.

I have seen that a period of mission in a church can be one of the most renewing, stimulating and fruitful phases in its life. I believe that churches should undertake mission at least every two or three years and that such missions should be part of realising their vision statement. Mission is a special time for Christians to move beyond the church walls and take the

Mission activities are a way of starting a conversation about Jesus...

gospel into the community. It enables them to meet non-Christians in a non-threatening way. Mission activities are a way of starting a conversation about Jesus and an opportunity for sharing his love.

Both leadership and congregation should really want a mission; both need to pledge their support to make the week's work worthwhile. If only a small number of the congregation are keen, it will result in a very poor mission. Using the techniques outlined in the previous chapter, it should be possible to arrive at a vision statement and to agree a number of priorities for evangelism in the local area. The leadership should discuss these goals, prioritise them and identify ways in which they might be accomplished. Faith-sharing should always be the central activity of the programme and at every stage of planning everyone should stop to ask, 'How is this helping us to fulfil Jesus' Great Commission?'

Over the following pages I have outlined guidelines for running a church-based mission. This is not a blueprint, but an example of how a church (perhaps supported by a visiting team) can engage in evangelism in their community.

Getting started

Naturally churches can engage in mission on their own, but my experience suggests that mission is more effective when the church hosts an 'away team'. The whole thing takes on a powerful dynamic when Christians from other churches come and help. When the same gospel is spoken by fresh voices it seems to cut more ice! An incoming team generates extra excitement and commitment locally. The mission becomes a two-way activity, with the churches hosting the event renewed and the visiting team members transformed by the experience.

It is important that the incoming team's leader visits the church well in advance, possibly about six months before the mission, for an honest time of sharing with the local minister, perhaps over a meal. It is crucial that there is a high degree of trust between team leader and minister. The visitor must pledge to support the minister both publicly and privately at all stages of the mission process or untold damage in the church could result.

During this early visit, probably during the evening, the visitor can meet with the church council or diaconate and discuss the local situation, view the aims and goals of the church, and participate in constructing a programme for the week of mission. The primary aim of the programme should be to empower everyone to share the good news about Jesus in the wider community. The secondary aim is to begin some of the 'new work' identified in the vision statement. This new work will need to be owned and fully supported by the congregation for at least 12 months after the mission has finished.

Mission programmes don't just happen; they come together after a great deal of planning and hard work. As the local leaders begin to prepare for the mission, they will constantly need to ask, 'Who? What? Where? When? How?' Deadlines must be set and individuals given specific areas of responsibility. Members of the congregation should be encouraged to own the mission from the earliest stages. A local 'facilities' committee could prepare for the visiting team's arrival, welfare, food and transport, while another group might take responsibility for the planning of the mission programme.

The more that people on the fringes of church life are involved in organising and implementing the programme, the more fruitful the mission will be. We always encourage the church to draw in people from outside to help with preparation for the mission and to facilitate things like barbecues, sports days and barn dances. The more people have a share in what's going on, the more likely it is that they will attend and come under the sound of the gospel.

Hosting a team

Any church hosting a team must accept that the team is not coming to do the work but to share as partners in mission. They must be willing to invest in the lives of each team member as well as to receive what each has to offer. Our experience has shown that missions are most effective when one team is commissioned to work with one congregation, no matter how small the congregation may be. The away team can encourage thinking for growth by the church and act as a catalyst for change.

It's helpful if the team come from a wide range of backgrounds and churchmanship. All they need in common is a love for Jesus and a desire to share the faith in contemporary ways. At Share Jesus, most of our teams have a mix of age groups, though some teams may be predominantly made up of one age group or another. We recognise that both younger and older people on the teams are today's Church, so we value their individual gifts and encourage them to grow in the Christian life. Having a range of age groups opens up wide possibilities. Suppose the mission programme includes working with local youth in a skateboard park. Young people on the team can join in the skateboarding; older people on the team can act as mentors or get involved in practical work such as building new skateboard slopes.

When the team arrives, the local people should host an event to welcome them. This first meeting provides an opportunity to commission everyone, including the home team, for witness together during the mission. The programme should provide lots of opportunities for the away team to pray and work with the home team so that there is no possibility of an 'us and them' culture developing. The aim is for everyone to be enriched by the partnership.

I am committed to this method of local church-based evangelism. After experiencing these missions in hundreds of different situations over the years in projects which have involved thousands of different team members, I can only say, 'It works!'

The results are threefold:

- ❖ The combined witness of the local church and the visiting team is very effective and lots of outsiders find real faith in Jesus.

- ❖ Through the mission, the local church gains confidence to move beyond its doors and make a diverse range of new contacts.

- ❖ The visiting team is changed for ever; God may lead some of them into Christian ministry as a result of their mission experience.

Looking back across 25 years of mission, the three most popular objectives identified by churches have been:

- ❖ raising the church's profile in the local community;

- ❖ beginning new work with teenagers;

- ❖ developing work with children.

These aims must be seen as part of a church's ongoing mission to its community. Taking these three aims as an example, I will highlight ways in which they could be given special emphasis during a week of local mission.

1 Connecting with the community

Christian witness in the community should always be accompanied by expressions of genuine service and a special time of mission is no exception. We must not only speak of the love of Jesus but demonstrate it in practical ways. Mission teams that visit the housebound, give a few hours of respite for carers or offer support for young parents will impact those who wouldn't be reached through an open-air meeting or gospel concert. In a tightly knit community, many people will get to hear that the visiting team's faith is not just about worship on Sunday but about practical service throughout the week. A mission team which operates as an evangelistic unit without a genuine spirit of service and compassion will lack credibility. In fact everything that a visiting team does should have the hallmark of Christlike compassion and love.

The door-to-door plan

Some techniques of door-to-door evangelism are a major turnoff. As I was writing this section, my doorbell rang and I was harassed for over twenty minutes by two earnest Jehovah's Witnesses. It was a textbook example of how to alienate and irritate someone. They were full of proof texts and they wanted to discuss one obscure Bible passage after another. There was a hardness about their presentation which irritated me and a frustrating unwillingness to hear what I was saying. They didn't leave me with any desire to meet them again or to go to their church. They hadn't taken time to cultivate a relationship and they didn't seem to care about me as a human being. They were simply reciting their patter.

However, I'm sure that it is still crucially important to visit people in their homes. One of the most effective ways of doing this is for the host church to find a way of visiting a selected band of housing regularly. Effective door-to-door witness should be an ongoing activity. It is far better to visit a hundred houses four times a year than a thousand houses once every five years! The goal of the church shouldn't be to drop thousands of leaflets through letterboxes, but rather to develop a dozen good relationships. A mission-minded church could engage in door-to-door witness by taking around special invitations or magazines several times a year. This could be repeated year by year until real relationships develop and the visits become part of local life. When this kind of groundwork has been laid, door-to-door work in the context of a mission is much more effective. The church member who has been visiting a certain street for a year or more can take one of the visiting team along to introduce them to the contacts they have already made on their round. This process brings a far greater possibility of success in inviting them to special outreach events than if a cold call is made.

The street dynamic

Some forms of Christian open-air witness are so embarrassingly bad, they have made me feel ashamed to be a Christian! But it doesn't have to be this way. I was in Leicester Square some time ago when I came across four young men who were singing barbershop in a superb and professional way. A crowd of around two hundred people gathered and as their show continued they featured spirituals such as 'Gonna lay down my sword and shield' and 'Dem dry bones'. The quality of their performance was as good as anything in the theatres across the street on Shaftesbury Avenue. Gradually they introduced short testimonies between the songs and the performance became a powerful and positive witness.

> **The street dynamic is about getting into the places where people are and becoming a part of their everyday lives.**

During local church missions we have used escapologists, street theatre performers, choirs, fire-eaters, unicyclists and even trapeze artists to draw a crowd and to introduce passers-by to the good news about Jesus.

The street dynamic is about getting into the places where people are and becoming a part of their everyday lives. Good street theatre and music can raise a church's profile in an area, publicise other events and become a contact point for meeting people and witnessing to them.

Community celebrations

Over recent years, our teams have developed programmes called 'Random acts of kindness' in which they do things for the local community with no other motive than to be kind. I once saw a team give out 500 ice-cold cans of Coke in a town centre one sweltering day in California, and I am sure it got people talking about the mission much more than would a glossy colour brochure.

I believe every church should try to organise regular community evangelistic events every year. When I was a minister, we used to organise an outreach bonfire party on November 5. We distributed tickets around the whole community and, besides a professional firework display, a massive bonfire and good music, there was an eight-minute 'epilogue' when people were munching their jacket potatoes. For the hundred local people standing in our church hall, it was a brief opportunity to reflect about life and faith. More importantly, it became a focus for our church's programme of evangelism and an opening for the congregation to introduce their friends to the church community.

This kind of programme can be the highlight of a mission. Where there is already a history of community events, it will be particularly effective. During the church missions Share Jesus coordinates, we sometimes organise community events such as a barn dance with a Christian caller, a summer barbecue with a guest singer, or a community sports day with a picnic tea, a bouncy castle and a visiting Christian sports personality. The presentation of the faith at these events only lasts for a few minutes and is usually integral to the programme of the day. Some missions we coordinate are more like community festivals and their witness may be based around a carnival procession, a series of sophisticated arts events, a country fair with sideshows, or a sequence of floral displays on biblical themes. I've seen teams constructing a replica of Noah's Ark on the back of a lorry, coordinating a Christian opera performance, organising a bookstall at a country fair, and putting together a flower show in a church sanctuary in a busy tourist centre. These are important opportunities for raising the church's profile, connecting with the local community and sharing literature about Jesus. When the church reconnects with the community in this way, we are able to speak to people where they are and gain a hearing which wouldn't be possible within the church walls.

2 Connecting with children

One of the greatest concerns about church life in the UK at present must be the declining numbers of children in attendance. A Church of England synod resolution passed in 2001 talked of the 'catastrophic decline over the past twenty years of the number of children and young people who are part of the worship and learning fellowship of the Church'. The resolution said that the long-term consequences of a society with little or no knowledge of Christianity are to 'make evangelism increasingly difficult'. Christian Research reports that for the first time in a millennium the Church is in touch with proportionately fewer children and young people than adults. While the majority of adults who attend church services today were in Sunday schools forty to sixty years ago, there is no such base being created at present on which the Church might draw in 2010 and after.

> **Church-based children's work has become a Cinderella ministry in the life of the church.**

Church-based children's work has become a Cinderella ministry in the life of the church. It is under-resourced and often unimaginative and ineffective. Yet many committed Christians took their first steps of faith when they were children.

Children are the emerging generation and we need to determine ways of reaching them which are contemporary and relevant. Very often our children's work uses techniques which were effective forty years ago but which have long-since passed their sell-by date. If we want to know where five- to ten-year-olds are at today, we need to watch Saturday morning TV. It takes a hi-tech, glitzy, multimedia, pop-orientated, celebrity-worshipping approach, with items lasting no more than three or four minutes. Mission among children will increasingly demand that we use hi-tech audio-visual resources and create imaginative programmes. Paper and crayons are no longer sufficient to attract their attention or speak to them about Jesus.

Understanding child development

It is important to understand something of child development, too. Children under six, for example, have random patterns of thinking and an inability to distinguish reality from fantasy. There's often confusion between miracles and magic. One of the most important things we can do for children of this age is to show a loving acceptance of them, even when they are disruptive. A child's world usually centres on their mum and/or dad, and we must learn how to relate to that world. Children under six generally experience faith. Through their experiences of security, responsiveness and openness they discover that God can be trusted; through being valued as an individual they find God's love; through the repair of friendships they discover repentance and reconciliation. The more we develop these important and positive experiences, the more we communicate the love of Christ.

The characteristics of 7–10-year-olds are very different. They have begun to think sequentially, are often hungry for knowledge and able to think in concrete terms. They have great loyalties to teams or groups and can generally distinguish reality from fantasy. The activities we devise must be stimulating, exciting and usually participatory. There is often the development of an 'affiliation faith' at this age, in which children discover commitment to Jesus by belonging to Christian groups.

Children aged over 11 often discover that their image is important. They identify closely with their peers, and may begin to ask big questions about meaning and purpose. They want to discover who they are. Abstract thinking and the questioning of authority are other hallmarks of this age group. This is the age for searching faith when questions need to be discussed and answers sought. We mustn't underestimate the seriousness of their quest for meaning.

In the ongoing mission of a local church we need to think creatively and radically. Do children's groups have to meet on a Sunday? How can mission programmes not only identify new groups of children, but also facilitate their nurture in exciting and relevant ways? One of the most effective children's clubs in the country meets at my local church every Thursday evening. The eighty children pay a modest amount to take part. There's a waiting list to join. Skilled drama teachers explore Bible stories using role play, drama games and other performing arts. The parents queue at the door to watch! We only gain a hearing from children if we invest high levels of energy and imagination in the programme.

A special week of mission provides a great opportunity for highlighting this kind of project, and many of our mission teams coordinate high-energy kids' clubs as part of their programme. It's all the more effective if this kind of work is already an ongoing part of church life. One word of important advice, however: It is crucial that the proper legal safeguards regarding adults working with children are properly adhered to. Everyone working with children should have a CRB (Criminal Records Bureau) check. And every church should have a carefully formulated child protection policy.

Some of the kids' mission activities we use at Share Jesus include the following:

Family devotions
This involves visiting families joining local families for team devotions each morning. The emphasis is on participation, with children of all ages taking part in music, drama, readings and quizzes.

Holiday clubs
These normally function each morning of a mission (during school holidays) from just after 10 in the morning to just before 12 noon. To comply with legal safeguards, we would recommend that clubs last less than two hours. The emphasis is on fun, games and creativity, often following the kind of interactive programmes published by Scripture Union.

Backyard clubs
Groups of local kids invite their friends to a backyard afternoon club in their own garden. Games and a barbecue are followed by a short Bible story, presented in an interactive way.

Evening activities
Campfires, sports nights, treasure hunts, wide games and team games are all good ways of getting children involved. Friendships established between leaders and children will lead many to faith in Jesus.

3 Connecting with youth

The youth scene is constantly changing and what was 'in' last week is surely 'out' this! Techniques which worked with teens last year probably won't work this year. Many of us have to face up to the fact that the era of the youth club with table tennis tables and dartboards is largely over.

However, mission among teens can very rewarding. Some of the neediest young people in our communities today are detached from any kind of regular youthwork. Some of them are missing out on regular schooling, while others have become strangers to normal home life. Yet these are some of the young people who are most open to the good news about Jesus. But to reach them is a costly business.

There are a number of interesting stages of adolescence which we should be aware of in our planning. The 11–14s phase is often the stage in which young people identify closely with small gangs of their peers. Then there is the transitional stage from 15 to 16 years – a time of very few close friends, crushes and moodiness. This is followed by the search for intimacy and a steady relationship.

One of the hallmarks of adolescence is a great feeling of insecurity, often connected with low self-esteem and anxieties about 'how I look'. It's an era of marked intellectual growth and of great pressure at school. There are major emotional developments, often accompanied by highs and lows, and there are the social developments connected with working through personal insecurities. Teens often begin to think independently and this can be the time for personal commitment to Jesus Christ and the choice of a life lived totally for him. Some youth activities we have found effective in recent years include the following:

Teen clubs

The programme can involve barbecues and night hikes, or sleep-overs in the church hall (with lots of leaders present!). All the activities should give plenty of space for relationship building.

Pioneer outreach

This is work among detached young people in the neighbourhood. Perhaps a gang of teens gathers in the local park each evening and at present there is no contact with the church. Hanging out with them and bringing them back to the church for coffee and burgers could be the start of ongoing contact and witness.

Nurture group

This involves a team-led study course for young people already in the orbit of church life. Leisure and fun activities mixed with interactive Bible study and fellowship are led by other teens on the team. They work on bringing young people to faith and releasing them into ministry.

Youth events

Christian rock bands, drama groups, dance companies and DJs can be given space to communicate the faith in contemporary ways, with young people given the opportunity to make a personal response to Jesus Christ.

Creating a mission programme

The mission programme needs to encourage creativity and fun and be a genuine expression of the love of Christ. The possibilities for the week are endless. I am constantly amazed at the way in which local churches evolve imaginative programmes for sharing the faith. The golden rule is that mission should never, ever, be boring. It should be inexpensive, creative and fun! The more mission events involve local people in preparation and participation, the more likely it is that they will be well supported.

Some practical ideas for what to include in your programme are included in the appendices at the end of this book.

3

THE
HEART
OF
EVANGELISM

8

A STRATEGY FOR EVANGELISM

Without doubt, prosperous urbanised countries such as the UK are the most difficult to evangelise. In such societies, we are faced with a decline in understanding about Christianity and a new generation that seems either hardened or oblivious to the claims of Jesus Christ. Our impact on society's belief systems is diminishing at a greater rate than our ability to make new church members. In just 25 years there has been a remarkable change in the popular perception of Jesus. Surveys have traced a decline in belief in the divinity of Christ, with increasing numbers seeing him as 'just a good man'. But, encouragingly, Jesus is still rated as a hero. A 2005 survey described him as a 'superhero' – in the same category as Florence Nightingale and footballer David Beckham!

We need to have an understanding of popular culture if we want to evangelise effectively. Many people's perspective on life is significantly shaped by the secular culture in which they live. If we want to be effective in mission, we must become familiar with the voices that are driving society today.

❖ The pluralist says, 'What's true for me is true, and what's true for you is true.' But Christianity teaches there is only one eternal truth, and only one true way. Ultimate truth is to be found in Jesus Christ.

❖ The modernist says, 'We're all cogs in a machine; we're all disposable. Nothing matters.' But the Christian argues that we are all precious to God, unique, loved and known by the One who gives us life.

- The relativist says, 'There are no rights and wrongs – it all depends on circumstances.' But our faith teaches us that there is right and wrong, good and evil – and we have the free will to choose the right way.

- The secularist says, 'Religion is a thing of the past. It has no relevance to life today.' But the Christian recognises that, whatever happens, God's kingdom will continue to grow and nothing in this world or the next can defeat it.

- The hedonist says, 'Eat, drink and be merry, for tomorrow we die.' But the Christian must remind him, 'After this comes judgement.'

- The futurist says, 'We're powerless to change anything. It's all pointless anyway.' But the Christian perspective is based in the almighty power of God and the belief that prayer changes things.

Ultimately, the Christian gospel looks at life in a totally different way to other world views. However, without some understanding of these perspectives, we will not be equipped to confront them. When witnessing to people, we are likely to face difficult questions and challenges to our faith. Evangelism is essentially a spiritual task: this is why we need others to pray for us so that we will be protected and empowered for the task.

Often the Church seems to have lost its way in its evangelism. I believe there are five key areas where the Church should direct its energy and resources in the highly secularised society of the West. These five areas should form the evangelistic agenda for mission in the third millennium.

1 Unreached people groups

Britain today is a mission field. The 2001 census counted 170 distinct religions. Although half of the British claim to believe in God and 72 per cent registered themselves in the census as Christians, some 66 per cent of the population have no actual connection with any church or religion. Between 1979 and 2005, half of all Christians stopped going to church on a Sunday. Church attendance in 2007 was estimated at around six per cent, declining at the rate of about two per cent per decade. We have an awesome task before us!

According to research, there are a number of people groups around the UK who are completely unreached by the Christian gospel. For example, there are tens of thousands of Asians from India and Bangladesh living in industrial areas with high unemployment, unable to communicate in English and lacking any Christian witness. There are hundreds of gypsies and travellers living on sites around the UK, with a high percentage of teens and children, and many of them feel rejected or marginalised by society. Although some have a Catholic background, many gatherings lack a Christian presence. You will be able to find other examples of unreached groups – possibly on your doorstep.

In towns and cities all over the country, increasing numbers of people fall outside the influence and witness of the Church. The continuing decline in the use of religious buildings for rites of passage such as the naming of children, weddings and funerals means that fewer and fewer people come into contact with the living community of believers. The urgent evangelistic task is for Christians to relocate to these areas and to witness among these unreached people through practical service and effective dialogue. Too many churches are so preoccupied with their own people or those on the fringes of their church life that they have no time or space to reach out to those who are completely unreached.

2 The task of apologetics

It can be stressful trying to handle questions about faith from young people! Surveys of the religious attitudes of secondary school pupils illustrate that the task of evangelism among teens is getting harder. We urgently need to discover ways to demonstrate that Christianity is credible and believable to this generation.

For many teenagers, science alone can explain spiritual phenomena, and science is perceived as the only key to all truth. Many young people believe that human beings are just complex chemical machines. I am convinced that a major task of evangelism is to address the apparent conflict between science and Christian faith.

Some years ago I undertook a fascinating tour called 'The Truth About Science' sponsored by the Evangelical Alliance. Together with astrophysicist and university chaplain Dr David Wilkinson, I visited some twenty towns and spoke to over 10,000 people. Each night we were accompanied by an internationally renowned scientist who was a committed Christian. It was a piece of mission work quite unlike anything I'd previously done. The people who came to the presentation tended to be quite intellectual, and many of them were not committed Christians. During the course of the evening, our presentation explored the relationship between science and faith, and argued that the Christian message is credible intellectually. We went on to explore the deep philosophical questions about origin and purpose which science throws up but which it cannot answer. The response was overwhelming. Hundreds of people from the audience took home literature about the Christian faith and many stayed behind for prayer.

As our society grows more secularised and the reservoir of Christian understanding evaporates, the evangelist will increasingly have to provide an apologetic for the Christian faith. We can no longer assume that people know the Christian story, let alone understand it. Increasingly, we will have to take our place in the marketplace of religious ideas and philosophical theories and make a credible defence of this faith which means so much to us.

3 Dialogue with people of other faiths

The growth of popular understanding about science, philosophy, comparative religion and psychotherapy has brought many other explanations of meaning into the public arena. The rise of non-Christian religion in the United Kingdom rose from half a million adherents in 1970 to over 3 million by the 2001 census and continues to rise.

Muslims are the largest religious group after Christians, with estimates varying between 1.5 and 2 million. There are approximately three-quarters of a million Hindus, a similar number of Sikhs and about 150,000 Buddhists. The presence of these and many other smaller non-Christian religious groups poses a great challenge for Christian mission. Many Christians are committed to welcoming and affirming these other faith communities; but they are neglecting the call to share Jesus Christ with them.

Dialogue is a fundamental part of any mission and its hallmarks must be genuine openness and interaction. Through talking to adherents of other faiths we can learn about their customs, religious awareness, values and assumptions about life. This dialogue is an integral part of the basic missionary task and, together with the development of long-term relationships, is the only way to win people of other faiths to Christ.

> **We need to ask God to give us a deep love and compassion for people of other faiths.**

In any such contact with people, it is imperative that we avoid unnecessary controversy and resist the temptation to quarrel or criticise. It is better to lose an argument than to lose a relationship. We are more likely to win someone for Christ through loving them than defeating them! However, we must take every opportunity to say what we believe and why we believe it. Personal testimony in such situations is important.

We need to ask God to give us a deep love and compassion for people of other faiths. Indeed, it may be appropriate for us to say sorry for the ways in which our imperialist culture has adversely affected their lives and the lives of their forebears. Over recent years hundreds of Christians have been following the old routes of the Crusades, apologising to Muslim people for the many injustices and cruel deeds done all those years ago in the name of Christ. They have encountered a warm and emotional response and sensed a new openness to begin again.

The Asian community is very hospitable. It is almost impossible to drop into an Asian home for just a few minutes. Hospitality is of enormous importance in the East and people are often thrilled when others visit them at home. Many Asians in the UK have little experience or understanding of British people as a people of prayer and devotion. Indeed, many of them see the Church as corrupt and Western culture as decadent. We have a lot of groundwork to do before any real sharing can begin.

One of our mission teams was working with an Asian Christian fellowship. They started up a series of 'English as a second language' home groups for women who were struggling with English speech and culture. The love, sharing and openness which the team found at these groups were remarkable and many deep conversations about Jesus took place. It was just this kind of multicultural situation in which the gospel first took hold and in which those who were hostile to Christianity were converted. The apostle Paul is a good example:

> I was personally unknown to the churches of Judea that are in Christ. They only heard the report: 'The man who formerly persecuted us is now preaching the faith he once tried to destroy.' And they praised God because of me.
>
> *Galatians 1:22–24*

I have met a number of people from other religious backgrounds in the UK who have accepted Christ as Saviour; they include Hindus, Buddhists, Jews and Muslims. Effective witness among people of other faiths *can* be done, as long as it is done in the right way and with the right sensitivity. I'm hoping for more of this in the coming years.

4 Witness to followers of alternative religions

The growth of interest in areas such as astrology, tarot cards, meditation and alternative medicine has brought a plethora of new religious perspectives. This plurality of meaning is the driving force behind secularism and runs contrary to Christian mission. Once the Church cornered the market on meaning, but now Christianity is seen as just one among many options. The Church has largely failed to understand this tide of new religious interpretations. Browse any high street bookstore and you will quickly discover that the religious section is dominated by New Age philosophy and spirituality, often under the label 'Body, Mind and Spirit'. A vast network of retail outlets devoted to these new philosophies is springing up all over the country.

A defining belief of many is that we are moving out of the age of Pisces and into the age of Aquarius. The spiritual energy flowing into the planet is focused along 'ley lines', and the places where these lines cross are called 'power points'. These energies are strongest when there is a full moon, and at the times of the equinoxes and solstices. The claim is that the new age will be an age of service, of living in harmony, of being attuned with the planet and with one another. It will be an age of groups and communities, of people living and working and learning together; an age in which the whole will be seen as greater than the sum of the parts – synergy. The underlying thesis of the movement is that you don't need to obey a God distinct from yourself because that idea is limiting; rather, you can do your own thing and connect with the divine power within yourself. In this way you will discover unlimited potential to transform yourself and the planet so that a new age of peace, light and love can begin.

These influences are penetrating our society on every level – the media, psychology, education, politics, business and medicine. Evangelists working among New Agers tell us that when they give their Christian testimony, the response is 'How lovely.'

We need to be very careful in our use of terminology. For the New Ager, being 'spiritual' refers to getting in touch with one's divine self rather than submitting to the Trinity. 'Christ' refers to a level of consciousness we can all attain rather than a title only fitting for Jesus of Nazareth. 'Atonement' refers to the idea that we are already in union with God rather than being reconciled to him through Jesus Christ. The New Ager is loath to discern any difference between their 'spiritual' experience and that of the committed Christian. If we point out the differences, they are likely to become angry and may even feel threatened. We must share Jesus with New Agers in a way that shows he is real to us but that is devoid of Christian jargon. The common starting points for dialogue are our shared appreciation for creation and shared sense of responsibility for the created order. We need to point out that while our God suffuses his creation, he is also a person who is apart from it.

One of our Share Jesus teams has had some experience of building bridges with a large community of New Agers living on Cool Mountain outside Cork in Southern Ireland. After an initially hostile reception, the team established a powerful Christian witness in the community. The witness was achieved largely through compassion, care and service. Slowly, residents grew more confident with the Christians among them and more open to talk about faith and spirituality. Through love and care, the team earned the right to talk about Jesus and to share the story of his work in their lives. A Christian prayer chapel was established in the community. Out of these experiences of working with New Agers I developed the six-week course Essence, to give participants insights into communicating the Christian faith in culturally relevant ways, and the book *A Closer Look at New Age Spirituality*.

> **Of all the forms of evangelism most appropriate for this millennium, I believe that community development is one of the most powerful and prophetic.**

5 Community-based evangelism

We have often seen evangelism as something cut off from the rest of life. When Jesus talked about mission in the world, he talked about the tiny piece of yeast which makes the bread rise, the pinch of salt that flavours everything it touches. Of all the forms of evangelism most appropriate for this millennium, I believe that community development is one of the most powerful and prophetic. It can also be one of the most effective. 'Community development' is a term used to describe a way not of providing things for people but of working with them so that they can help themselves. In this kind of mission, Christians become involved in helping people to achieve their full potential. The concern is to develop the whole person: their spiritual, emotional, physical and social needs and their sense of well-being. This is a long-term programme of evangelism which begins by meeting people in their needs, hopes and aspirations. When this happens the church becomes known as a place of belonging, of caring, of growth for individuals. Eventually it becomes an integral part of the community.

Over the last few years several of our missions have been based in urban priority areas and have adopted the community development model for mission as their guide. The results have been exciting. One team outside Glasgow developed a drop-in centre with a group of single mums in a tower block – a centre which became known for caring, service and Christian witness. In another urban priority area, where the council was offering council houses for 50 pence (if you spent £25,000 to renovate them!), a retired couple moved in to begin a programme of community development among people who felt disenfranchised and powerless. By working alongside their neighbours in many caring projects, they demonstrated the power and integrity of the Christian gospel.

On a needy estate, people don't normally go to church. As the church engages in community development, it helps people develop new ideas of what Church is about. Gradually, new relational networks are established and people who have had little or no contact with Christians begin to understand what Christians believe and why. In this way Christians can engage in the pressing issues of the estate and work alongside the local people in tackling them. The signs of the kingdom are acted out in everyday life and Jesus Christ is celebrated not only in word but in deed. Experience has shown that the community soon begins to see that the gospel of Jesus really is good news for the poor, relevant to real life and real needs. The community development style of mission can operate in suburbs, small towns, even in villages. I believe it to be one of the most effective ways of reaching a whole community with the gospel.

Ultimately, the local church should be like yeast in dough or salt in food. It will have a much greater long-term effect if it is immersed in the ongoing life of the local community rather than by doing hit-and-run missions. Evangelism is about living as Christ within the community. The slow but dynamic influence of a small group of people who really believe in Jesus can eventually transform a village, town, city – even a nation! The future is full of possibilities and Christians are called to look beyond the needs of maintaining their denominational structures to the bigger vision of winning others for Christ. As we live the life that he has called us to, both individually and corporately, we will begin to see people and places beginning to change. I believe he can use us to do things for him beyond our wildest imagining.

A vision for growth

Over the centuries, the Christian community has become an ever larger proportion of the world's population. In 1430 only one per cent of the world's population was Christian; today it's more like thirty per cent! The Christian Church is growing faster than the world's birth rate! Why, then, have so many Christians in the West seemingly lost their confidence in the gospel? They are unwilling to die for their faith, but would rather deny it. Many recognise that evangelism is a very costly and demanding activity and so choose to keep their faith to themselves.

> Then James and John, the sons of Zebedee, came to him. 'Teacher,' they said, 'we want you to do for us whatever we ask.'
>
> 'What do you want me to do for you?' he asked.
>
> They replied, 'Let one of us sit at your right and the other at your left in your glory.'
>
> 'You don't know what you are asking,' Jesus said. 'Can you drink the cup I drink or be baptised with the baptism I am baptised with?'
>
> 'We can,' they answered.
>
> Jesus said to them, 'You will drink the cup I drink and be baptised with the baptism I am baptised with...'
>
> *Mark 10:35–39*

The cup, the towel, the yoke

There are many pieces of equipment a contemporary evangelist may need for his task: a decent car, a good website, a business card. But the most essential equipment for anyone with a vision for evangelism is the cup that Jesus offered – the cup of suffering. His whole life was committed to suffering in obedience to his Father's will and to caring for those who suffer. Evangelism is far more credible when Christians are willing to enter into the sufferings of the world.

Evangelism is far more credible when Christians are willing to enter into the sufferings of the world.

Preparing a radio programme for transmission a couple of days after the horrific shooting of many innocent children in Dunblane, Scotland, I called Victim Support in the town for an interview. After a couple of minutes the leader of this agency in Dunblane asked, 'Is that wee Robbie?' I agreed that my name was Rob! She went on to tell me that she had re-committed her life to Christ at a meeting I'd led in Scotland. As part of her new commitment to Jesus she had got involved with Victim Support and now found herself at the centre of one of her nation's greatest tragedies.

The second essential piece of equipment for today's evangelist is the towel of service.

> Jesus called them together and said, 'You know that those who are regarded as rulers of the Gentiles lord it over them, and their high officials exercise authority over them. Not so with you. Instead, whoever wants to be come great among you must be your servant, and whoever wants to be first must be slave of all. For even the Son of Man did not come to be served, but to serve, and to give his life as a ransom for many.'
> *Mark 10:42–45*

During Easter People in 1999, I glimpsed through my hotel window the thousands of delegates walking expectantly down the street towards the massive Bournemouth International Centre. As I watched, I could hear the television news reporter describing the alarming and horrific pictures of the Kosovan refugees trekking wearily towards Albania. It seemed to me that what we were doing in our great evangelical celebrations was anathema if we were unresponsive to what was happening in the rest of the world. Later that evening I went onto the platform and told four thousand people how I felt. Between 9am and 9pm the following day, Easter People collected over 14 tons of aid, purchased and insured a lorry, found two drivers and sent the precious cargo off to a church swamped with refugees in southern Albania. They also collected £30,000 and despatched it within hours to relief agencies for specific projects among the refugees.

We have 'done evangelism' at Easter People for many years. Open-air meetings, posters, free tickets to musicals, distribution of tracts and street theatre… but nothing in all my experience had such an evangelistic impact on the town as this one act of kindness. As hundreds of people queued to donate blankets, pillows and cooking utensils, reporters from newspapers, TV and radio stations all over the region began to show up. Hundreds of townsfolk joined the queue and the news of our effort spread like wildfire through hotels and shops as we became inundated with gifts for our relief effort. This one good deed did more to convince the townsfolk that our faith meant something real to us than any sophisticated media presentation. We can be big on words – but if we are short on deeds our message sounds hollow and empty.

The final piece of equipment for the evangelist to take with him for the task is the yoke of obedience. Essentially, evangelism is about obedience – total submission to Jesus Christ, willingness to go where he sends us and to speak on his authority. My vision for the evangelists of the new millennium is that each will carry with him or her the cup, the towel and the yoke – symbols of true servanthood and sacrifice.

What has always moved me about the story of James and John and Jesus' challenge to them is that history proved they were listening! We read in the book of Acts that King Herod had 'James, the brother of John, put to death with the sword'. James was the first of the twelve apostles to suffer martyrdom and was killed during a time of Christian persecution under Herod Agrippa in AD 44. If we really would share Jesus in the twenty-first century, we follow in the footsteps of tens of thousands of others who have gone before us, people like James who paid the ultimate price for their faithfulness to the message.

I know that God will continue to raise up new generations of Christians to stand firm in the gospel and take every opportunity to share Jesus in the ever-growing work of building God's kingdom. The big question is, will you be a part of this strategy? Will you share in the greatest work we can ever do on earth – leading others to the Saviour, Jesus Christ?

9

A BURDEN FOR EVANGELISM

The first proper mission I ever took part in was a harrowing experience. I was a student at Cliff College, a Bible college in Derbyshire's Peak District. We were sent out on our first mission to a rather spartan area near Sheffield called Gleadless. I was dispatched by the team leader to go out onto the streets and find young people to come and see a film in the church hall. The streets were empty and the drizzling rain swept across the urban sprawl. Eventually I came across a fish and chip shop with a crowd of leather-clad teenagers standing inside eating their chips. Rather nervously I invited them to see the film, which featured a rather young Cliff Richard, I remember. To my amazement, they agreed to come.

I sauntered back to the church and about half an hour later the motorbikes roared up and they came inside. They sat on a table at the back of the room chewing gum and giggling but no one seemed to mind too much. At the end of the evening the evangelist made an appeal and, to my utter astonishment, one of the bikers went forward and knelt at the front. He was led off to a counselling room where the gospel was shared and prayers were said. We said goodnight to him and his gang and looked forward to welcoming them back the next day. That was not to be. Within two hours the young man was dead, killed in a tragic motorcycle accident.

I have never forgotten it. From this earliest experience of evangelism I came to recognise that Christian mission is not a game, not something the Church does to make up its numbers. It's a hallowed privilege, a commission none of us can honestly evade.

Time and again across the years I have thought of that lad and my brief but important conversation with him on his last night on earth. It convinced me that evangelism is the Church's most urgent task. In telling others we fulfil the very heart of the Church's mission. The decisions made as a result are made for eternity. God forgive us if we don't tell others, for we miserably fail them and deny them the greatest opportunity of all – an opportunity to form a relationship with Jesus Christ, the Saviour of the world.

It is easy for the work of evangelism to become just another duty or yet something more we've got to do.

It is easy for the work of evangelism to become just another duty or yet something more we've got to do. Whenever I lead teams on mission, I usually gather them together on the first evening for a private prayer session. I explain that without a God-given love for the place where we are on mission and for the people among whom we are working, we will miss the true significance of what we are doing. In mission after mission and year after year, I've known the Lord give us that love. Sometimes it has been almost tangible – a heart-gripping kind of love flowing out in service, care and compassion. If we are to be effective in evangelism, we each need that kind of love, a love so profound that it expresses God's love for the world and humanity. As we enter into the enormity of this love, we share the privilege of becoming ambassadors for Christ.

Felt needs

It is easy for Christians to forget what it's like not to have faith. We may have to cast our mind back many years to recall what life was like before we met Jesus. The comfort, strength, meaning and joy that our relationship with him has brought us have often become such an integral part of who we are that we take it for granted! In his letters to the first Christian churches, the apostle Paul often had to remind his readers what life used to be like before their conversion:

> ... remember that at that time you were separate from Christ, excluded from citizenship in Israel and foreigners to the covenants of the promise,

> without hope and without God in the world.
>
> *Ephesians 2:12*

If we are to be effective in evangelism, we need to think ourselves into the feelings, lifestyle and circumstances of the people we are trying to reach. Part of sensing a burden for others is to empathise with their circumstances and understand their situation. The gospel is most relevant where it matches another person's need. It teaches that each person is unique and of incalculable personal value. In the words of Francis Schaeffer and Everett Koop in *Whatever Happened to the Human Race?* (Marshall, Morgan & Scott, 1980):

> Each man, woman and child is of great value, not for some ulterior motive such as self gratification, or wealth or power or as a 'sex object' or for the 'good of society' – but because of his or her origin. God has created every human being in His own image.

What, then, are some of the greatest felt needs that people have in contemporary society today, and how can we begin to feel a burden for them?

Security

John Naisbitt, an influential researcher of contemporary trends in American society and author of *Megatrends: Ten New Directions Transforming Our Lives* (Grand Central Publishing, 1988), has written:

> As a society we are moving from the old to the new and we are still caught in motion. Caught between eras we experience turbulence, during turbulent times people need structure not ambiguity in their lives. This demand for structure will increase ... people are looking for something to hang on to, not something to debate.

It's true. Millions are caught up in a whirl of mass redundancy and relocation, of marriage break-up (the average marriage lasting 11 years in 2004), of uncertain health and stressful situations in parenting. And much more. Our society is a roller coaster of constant change and people are looking for something solid to hang on to.

The search for security has featured in the writings of many famous philosophers. Boswell, the eighteenth-century philosopher, kept asking where the 'centre of a man' is. He was looking for the point of 'steadfastness' from which his needs could at last be known. Christians believe that the fixed point is Jesus – the Alpha and the Omega, the first and the last, the start and the finish. He's the One in whom everything finds its proper place. In a society looking for something to hang on to, we can point people to Jesus, who is the source of all security and the rock-solid foundation on whom we can safely build our lives.

Meaning

We live in a materialistic society in which most of us are intent on acquiring more and more things. Many sociologists have noted how unsatisfying this consumerism is. Contemporary advertising persuades us not only to purchase things for their intrinsic usefulness, but as a means of reinforcing our personal identity. Unfortunately, in this process, the thing which we strive to own can own us. In the words of humanist psychoanalyst Eric Fromm (*To Have or To Be?*, Cape, 1996):

> I am not myself, I am what I have. My property constitutes myself and my identity. The thought in the statement 'I am I' is 'I am I because I have X, Y and Z' – ie all natural objects and persons to whom I relate myself through my power to control them, to make them permanently mine. In the having mode there is no alive relationship between me and what I have. It and I have become things, and I have it – because I have the force to make it mine. But there is also a reverse relationship – it has me, because my sense of identity rests upon my having it.

The hedonistic pleasure-seeking materialism which envelops much of our society is leaving many people feeling empty and lost. They are looking for deeper meaning. Where they can't find it, feelings of futility and despair can come to dominate. The suicide rate in the UK is giving cause for concern. There are 4700 suicides each year and many more are attempted. Suicide is currently the most common cause of death for teenage boys 15-plus. Telephone helplines tell their own story, with hundreds of thousands each year calling the Samaritans, Alcoholics Anonymous or Relate.

The things which we own can never really add meaning to our lives. Only a living relationship with Jesus Christ can do that. He created us, he knows us and he sees the potential of what we could become. Our burden for those who feel like this must drive us to communicate his love. Only through their connection with him will they discover real purpose for their existence and uncover the rich potential he has for their lives.

Spirituality

Many young people are absorbing themselves in the current clubbing and binge-drinking culture in their search for a spiritual dimension to life. But young people are not alone in this quest for meaning. In a highly pressured world, where success is everything and those who are unsuccessful are considered inferior, many are looking for escape. People of all ages are exploring a growing number of new forms of popular spirituality. This exploration is one of the most significant characteristics of new millennium

We must learn to talk about prayer, worship and our sense of God with more conviction and confidence.

society. Seventy two per cent of people now believe that 'Religion no longer provides the answers to many of today's problems' according to The Henley Centre (research consultancy) in 2000. We should not be ashamed, therefore, of talking about Christian spirituality. We must learn to talk about prayer, worship and our sense of God with more conviction and confidence. The apostle Paul demonstrated this confidence when he addressed the council of the city of Athens!

> 'Men of Athens! I see that in every way you are very religious. For as I walked around and looked carefully at your objects of worship, I even found an altar with this inscription: TO AN UNKNOWN GOD. Now what you worship as something unknown I am going to proclaim to you.'
> Acts 17:22,23

The good news is that Jesus accepts us as we are. When he comes into our lives, he can make us whole in body, mind and spirit. In Jesus we have a Saviour who gives us a sense of purpose and direction like none other.

Suffering

If someone is hurting emotionally, even the simplest presentation of the Jesus story should relate to their pain. We must learn how to demonstrate that our faith has helped us in our own difficulties and that knowing Jesus has given us chinks of light in the dark places of our journey through life. When I'm talking to someone recently bereaved, for instance, I often talk about my own experience of grief following the death of my mum and how my faith helped me through that. When I'm talking to someone in hospital, I try to draw on my experiences of illness and show how prayer has been a strength and support to me. Effective Christian witness always takes account of suffering and applies our faith story to the circumstances of the person we are witnessing to.

Loneliness

Research projects support the idea that there is a rising tide of loneliness. I was given some insight into this issue when I attended a seminar at a national television conference which revealed the findings of research done on the popularity of 'soaps'. Every week these programmes top the ratings, with millions watching shows like EastEnders, Coronation Street and Emmerdale. Viewer interaction with the characters featured in the storylines can be astonishing; the actors may receive hundreds of letters of condolence, birthday cards, even hatemail each week. Researchers told the conference that the reason for the popularity of such shows is that people are hungry to belong to a community and desperate for relationship. They express these deeply felt needs in their addiction to imaginary worlds and fictional characters. It's a lonely world.

According to sociologist Yvonne Roberts, men are particularly prone to loneliness. In her detailed survey of conversations of men aged 35, she discovered that while they say a lot, they reveal practically nothing about themselves. In *Man Enough* (Chatto & Windus, 1984), she writes:

> Men seem to spend a lot of time talking to each other, but very little time actually saying anything which touches on the reality of the lives that they are living ... step outside the formula, and talk about emotions, fear, failure, love, joy – and you become a loner, a bit 'soft' – less of a man.

A man might be facing bankruptcy, terminal cancer or marriage breakdown, but is unlikely to tell his drinking pals anything about it. When asked how he's feeling, he will simply say, 'Everything's fine.' There's plenty of communication but little relationship.

There is loneliness among students, too. A counselling website for Cambridge University explains:

> Leaving home and coming to university involves a number of changes: in lifestyle, work patterns, and degree of independence. The accumulated effects of these can make people feel uncertain of what to do or how to be. Social insecurities can then creep in, even in people who normally feel quite socially adept. So, for some, loneliness is a new and disconcerting experience, while for others it is more familiar, but may now be accompanied by disappointment that university has not brought a hoped for change.

We live in a society desperate for relationships and our gospel is full of good news about relationships. When we become Christians, we find a new friend in Jesus Christ – someone who loves us, accepts us and remains with us. When we become friends of Jesus, we discover a whole new friendship network of belonging in the life of the Church.

The pilgrimage

Christianity isn't a religion designed only to help us at church! It's a faith that brings meaning, strength, direction and healing to the whole of life. It fulfils the needs we have all experienced at one time or another.

I used to believe that there were just two kinds of people: believers and non-believers. Over more than twenty years engaged in front-line evangelism, however, I have to say that I find the process a lot more complicated now than I used to. Many people are making a journey of faith, whether they recognise it or not. They may be at the starting block or well along the track. We need to discover where they are along the road if we are to move them forward in their faith journey.

One day I challenged my secretary about the amount of time our staff were giving to the postman who brought the mail to our office each morning. I was getting irritated by his chit-chat and the evident enthusiasm with which he delivered our letters each morning. She drew herself up to her full height and peered at me over the top of her spectacles. 'Recently,' she said, 'you told us that we should be witnesses for Christ where we are. I've got a problem. We're all Christians in this office. Who else can I witness to?'

I felt thoroughly and deservedly chastened. Shortly afterwards the postman came in with a terrible confession: he had lost a registered letter. Our office team readily gathered round him, laid hands on his sack and prayed for the lost letter. When he returned the next day, lost letter in hand, we all rejoiced together. Later, when I was preaching to over two thousand people in Westminster Central Hall, I looked across the bright beam of the spotlights to the faces of the people in the front row. There was the postman, smiling in warm affirmation. I believe we helped to move him on in his pilgrimage of faith.

The Engels Scale was devised by missionaries in South America as a means of identifying the process of evangelism. As they researched the response of the people with whom they were working, they developed this scale to illustrate that people are at different levels:

+5	Stewardship
+4	Communion with God
+3	Conceptual and behavioural growth
+2	Incorporation into Body
+1	Post-decision evaluation
	NEW BIRTH
-1	Repentance and faith in Christ
-2	Decision to act
-3	Personal problem recognition
-4	Positive attitude towards Gospel
-5	Grasp implications of Gospel
-6	Awareness of fundamentals of Gospel
-7	Initial awareness of Gospel
-8	Awareness of supreme being, no knowledge of Gospel

Some have added earlier stages such as 'Some awareness of God' and 'No awareness of God'. Yes, there really are people who have never sensed the presence of God or considered that he might exist. Some have a slight awareness, perhaps through the changing seasons or the beauty of the created world.

When I started to use the Engels Scale in my own work, I stopped seeing people as just 'believers' or 'non-believers' and began to see them as travellers at different stages of a journey. I began to view them not as 'in' the kingdom of God or 'out' of it, but as 'on the way'. This realisation affected the way I spoke to people and the way I sought to share my faith with them. Some of the detached street kids our teams witness to move from having 'no awareness of God' to 'some awareness of God' and that can be significant progress.

This kind of thinking has transformed my view of evangelism. I used to try to lead people to Christ in one fell swoop, but now I see evangelism as helping people to take the next step in their journey of faith towards discovering Jesus. God lives on a bigger map than us and I don't believe that he wants the good news about Jesus delivered in such a way that it alienates people and disregards their circumstances. The Lord is working with people before we come on the scene, and he'll be working with them long after we have gone!

Moving people along the Engels Scale is the responsibility of the Body of Christ working under his Lordship. God's way is not to ask us to put our foot in a stranger's door to try and move them ten points in ninety seconds! No, if our witness only moved someone one point along the Engel scale, with that witness reinforced by other members of the Body of Christ whom that person met day by day, it would be so much more effective. Thousands would be finding Christ every week and the Body of Christ would be functioning as it was meant to function!

Lifestyle evangelism

Sometimes Jesus called people to leave everything and follow him. In simple obedience, people like Peter, James and John left their boats, their fishing business, their home town, their family and their loved ones to take to the open road with him. But there were others – many others – whom Jesus didn't invite to join him. To them, he simply said, 'Go home.'

The wild Gerasene demoniac whom Mark tells us about in his Gospel, living among the caves and tombs far from civilisation, was considered dangerous and insane. He was chained up, but often managed to break free. What a sight he must have been – flowing hair, unkempt beard, wild eyes, raw and bleeding from the many cuts he'd inflicted on himself. When Jesus healed him, casting a host of demons out of him into a herd of pigs, he was clean, clothed and in his right mind.

> As Jesus was getting into the boat, the man who had been demon-possessed begged to go with him. Jesus did not let him, but said, 'Go home to your family and tell them how much the Lord has done for you, and how he has had mercy on you.'
>
> Mark 5:18,19

When he returned home, that man would have made a profound impression on everyone. The transformation in his life spoke more clearly about the power of Jesus Christ than a thousand articulate sermons. He went home and lived the transformation.

Most of us haven't experienced quite such a dramatic testimony of the Lord's dealing with us, but who we are and what he has done for us still speaks more clearly than anything else. The way we live, the people we are and the priorities we make will all be powerful aspects of our Christian witness to others. This is at the heart of lifestyle evangelism. If there are aspects of our life that the Lord needs to sort out, it's important that we allow him to do so.

One time when Jesus was passing through Jericho, he came across a small man hiding in a tree. Zacchaeus wasn't the most popular guy in town; he worked for the Romans – the enemy – and would have been considered a traitor. Not only that, he was known as a dishonest taxman, reputed to be cooking the books. When Jesus visited him and led him to salvation, Zacchaeus didn't leave town to follow Jesus. No! He said, 'Look, Lord! Here and now I give half of my possessions to the poor, and if I have cheated anybody out of anything, I will pay back four times the amount.' We can only begin to imagine the impact such a decision would have made on the small community of Jericho. It would have been the talk of the town! The generous care of the taxman would have touched the lives of many. Like Zacchaeus, we must learn what it means to witness where we live, in deed as well as in word.

When Jesus met the Samaritan woman by the well, the conversation he had with her left her deeply moved. She raced back to her village and gossiped the good news! 'Come and see the man who told me everything I have ever done!' Through what she said, and the excitement and conviction with which she said it, some believed in Jesus. It's not enough just to share the good news of Jesus through our changed lives and our good deeds. Like the woman, we must go home and tell others. There are opportunities all around us, and daily we should pray for openings to speak about Jesus and tell of what he has done in our lives.

One night I was travelling on a long plane journey with a well-known Christian leader and speaker, Roger Forster. It seemed never-ending, and the selection of movies was dire. We couldn't sleep, so we talked and talked. After some time, Roger asked me if I was related to a man called Frost who had once been a London City Missioner around Battersea. I explained that this was my great-grandfather. Roger told me of the love and grace which shone from this man, and how he'd collected a tribe of children each Sunday to take to Sunday School. Roger Forster was one of them. I never met my great-grandfather, but his witness continues through one of my contemporary heroes, Roger Forster.

When you buy a stick of seaside rock, you will often discover that the name of the resort is stamped throughout the whole stick. Break it in the middle, at the end or anywhere else and you will find the name 'Blackpool' or whatever. In the same way, our faith must penetrate every aspect of our life – work, leisure, the family and the community. Lifestyle evangelism is one of the most powerful forms of all Christian witness. As people see our relationship with Christ in the cut and thrust of everyday life, we must pray that they come to understand what he means to us.

Many years ago, I was at a camp for inner-city kids. One of the rough, tough lads recommended for the camp was a young teenager called David. One night, beside the dying embers of a campfire, I overheard one of the leaders, Barrie, ask David if he would like to become a Christian, and the young lad nodded.

More than twenty years later, I sat in a church in Brixton, inner London, and joined in one of the most powerful funeral services I've ever been part of. The church was packed to capacity, with chairs down the aisles and the doorways crowded with those who couldn't get in. In the coffin carried into the church was the body of David, who had died of a blood disorder. Barrie from the youth camp was walking slowly behind the coffin as it moved awkwardly down the aisle.

In true Caribbean style, the funeral was relaxed and informal, with laughter, tears and singing. Many people stood up to praise God for David's life and testimony. He had impacted the area in powerful ways. During his short life, David had accepted the faith, become an ordained minister and lived his witness in one of the most difficult cultural settings for Christian mission. At the end of the service I stood with hundreds of people and watched the cortège drive away. I was moved with emotion, remembering how this one life was transformed by Christ and how, in turn, this one life had affected hundreds of other lives – all because Barrie had a burden for evangelism.

10

A VISION FOR EVANGELISM

We live in a success-driven society. In practically every profession in recent years there has been a new emphasis on productivity and quality control. In many disciplines the emphasis has been on quantity. How many surgical operations did you perform? How many more insurance policies did you sell this month compared to last? How are your students performing in examinations compared to the national average?

This kind of thinking can permeate the life of the Church, especially the field of evangelism. Even the most credible Christian evangelistic organisations sometimes become over-concerned with growth targets, new membership indices, response percentages and conversion rates. When a team of British Methodist ministers visited a church in Korea, they were staggered to discover that the church leaders presented a new car each year to 'the most successful soul-winner' in the congregation! Evangelists can easily be seen as the sales force of the Church, and programmes of mission and evangelism judged as effective solely by their ability to produce results quickly.

While I have no problem with the concept of effectiveness in mission, or of using our resources in the most productive ways, I don't believe that success-driven evangelism is biblical. Many Christians are discouraged about their witness and feel that they are not successful. I have met mission-minded Christians who have slogged on, year after year, and grown tired and fed up because of apparently poor results. Their initial enthusiasm has dwindled because of lack of new converts. I can empathise with these feelings because I have been there myself. I entered the ministry with all the sensitivity of a bull in a china shop! I flew around trying to do everything myself, hoping to bring the world to Christ in a week or two. After a few months I was completely exhausted and somewhat disheartened.

One day an older and wiser minister came to see me. He told me that I was trying to do too much, too soon. He showed me that I had been setting targets for myself which were not the Lord's and goals that God was not asking me to reach.

The Bible sets out some clear principles for the process of evangelism. If we embark on mission without understanding them, we are likely to end up looking like failed used-car salesmen. Let's look at some of them.

Sow, even when the odds are against you

The task of evangelism can seem pretty hopeless. A witnessing congregation can feel pathetic and outnumbered a thousand to one by those in the local area who have little or no interest in the Christian faith.

One summer I went to help a friend bring in the harvest on his Yorkshire farm. I had no idea what harvesting would be like. As I learned how to drive the tractor, throw bales of straw into the barn and unclog the baler, I began to realise just how stressful an occupation farming can be. Yet each night Richard and I would stagger back to the farmhouse covered in sweat and grime, but with a glow of satisfaction that 'all was safely gathered in'.

One day we had to take a trailer full of oilseed rape from the combine harvester in the field to the large storage silo in the farmyard. I rode through the village on the back of the trailer piled high with shifting seed. Holding on to the swaying trailer as we went, I gradually sank lower and lower into the cargo until my wellingtons and trousers were filled with the oily black stuff and I couldn't move. It was not a pleasant experience! When we arrived at the farmyard, my friend lowered a large black suction pipe into the trailer and we watched as the seed was sucked up into the silo. He sighed: 'This stuff is amazing – we sow it in pounds and reap it in tons!' Eventually I was released! As I watched the crop gradually disappearing,

I remembered the parable of the mustard seed and understood the full force of its meaning for the first time. In each mustard seed of the gospel there is incalculable growth potential, and its prospects for growth far exceed our capacity to understand how it happens.

> [Jesus said:] 'The kingdom of heaven is like a mustard seed, which a man took and planted in his field. Though it is the smallest of all your seeds, yet when it grows, it is the largest of garden plants and becomes a tree, so that the birds of the air come and perch in its branches.'
> *Matthew 13:31,32*

This parable really came alive for me when I visited Gwennap Pit in Cornwall. Every year, thousands of Methodists from around the world visit this large amphitheatre situated miles from anywhere. It is the site where John Wesley used to preach to the Cornish tin miners in the open air, and where hundreds of them found Jesus Christ as Saviour. An actor dressed as John Wesley preached in the arena, surrounded by young Methodists from all over the world. It was a powerful reminder of Wesley's preaching ministry and of the way the Lord used him to bring revival. As I gazed around at that great crowd, I was overwhelmed by the thought that the preaching of one man could result in a worldwide denomination numbering hundreds of millions of people. It was a powerful demonstration that the growth potential in any seed of the gospel is greater even than that of a mustard seed!

When just one life is transformed and redeemed by the power of Jesus Christ, that life has the potential to influence thousands more.

Our approach to evangelism, therefore, is different from that of a sales force for a new product or an advertising agency selling a new brand. The gospel of Jesus Christ, when faithfully sown, has its own growth potential. 'Success' and 'sales volume' is not primarily generated by the evangelist – it is inherent in the gospel itself. When just one life is transformed and redeemed by the power of Jesus Christ, that life has the potential to influence thousands more. The gospel is not some inanimate object like a new car or a soda drink which, once purchased, quickly depreciates or is consumed. No! The Christian message has a power within it which can transform individuals, their families, their communities and their nations. Its effect and influence grow with the years.

When we embark on the work of evangelism we must recognise that every seed of good news we sow has the potential within it to transform not just one life but thousands of lives. Though we sow in pounds, we will eventually reap in tons.

Sow, even when you can't see results

Our society is mesmerised by performance indicators, growth graphs and return on investment. The task of evangelism can never be quantified in such terms. The growth of faith is often silent, immeasurable – even sometimes seemingly non-existent. Only God knows the final figures or the bottom line. The growth of the Christian Church is seldom spectacular. It is often unremarkable, like new shoots peeping out of the earth in springtime.

Several years ago I joined hundreds of other Christians on an Easter Monday pilgrimage organised by the Anglican Diocese of Kent. Hundreds of people walked across the Downs to Canterbury Cathedral, following in the footsteps of Augustine, the early Christian missionary, whose monks evangelised England from AD 597. During the service each one of us was given a small unlit candle. Near the end of the worship the archbishop lit his candle and explained that this symbolised the light of the gospel which Augustine brought to England. Gradually the flame was passed from candle to candle down the long nave, until thousands of them were alight.

I was standing at the back of the cathedral during this silent activity, and it was breathtaking to watch. Slowly but surely the light from the candles lit up the dark recesses of the cathedral as it flickered towards me. When the candles were all alight, we lifted them high and the whole cathedral was a blaze of light. The archbishop used this as a poignant reminder that the light of the gospel affecting our nation over so many centuries started from small flickering beginnings. The gospel's growth has been silent, unspectacular; but over the centuries the effect has been staggering. Lighting my own candle and passing on the flame reminded me that I must play my part in a never-ending process of sharing Jesus.

Augustine wasn't the only evangelist of his time. Every year thousands of people from all over the world visit the tiny Scottish island of Iona to thank God for the life and work of an early missionary called Columba. He started to evangelise Scotland with a dozen missionaries from Iona in AD 563. From this base he planted churches all over Scotland. Again, what began as something very small has had far-reaching and powerful effects throughout history.

When Robert Raikes was a young man living in eighteenth-century Gloucester, he walked through the town square one Sunday afternoon and saw the children playing on the street. They were illiterate, ill-disciplined and totally outside the life of the Church. Raikes despaired of this situation and felt that the future for these children was hopeless. But then he heard a voice saying to him, 'Try, try, try.' He was so convinced that this was a divine commission, he started a Sunday school to help children read the Bible. Little did he know that what started as a small initiative to reach a handful of youngsters would develop into a worldwide movement touching the lives of millions of young people and bringing countless thousands to Christ.

I have attended Sunday schools in prosperous California and in struggling mud hut villages in Africa. I have spoken at Sunday schools in sophisticated Singapore and on banana plantations in the Caribbean. The seed which he sowed has become a harvest.

[Jesus said:] 'A man scatters seed on the ground. Night and day, whether he sleeps or gets up, the seed sprouts and grows, though he does not know how. All by itself the soil produces corn – first the stalk, then the ear, then the full grain in the ear. As soon as the grain is ripe, he puts the sickle to it, because the harvest has come.'
Mark 4:26–29

For more than ten years my wife and I ran youth groups in our home. We had many great times. It wasn't always easy, however, and there were some Sunday nights when we used to wonder whether we were wasting our time. At some stage each one of our youth groups had its problems, but one group in South London was a particular pain. Sometimes I felt as if the kids were taking their teenage rebellion out on me rather than their parents! For a time my wife and I came to dread Sunday evenings. Every suggestion was opposed, every discussion starter ridiculed. There were times when we felt like giving up altogether. It constantly baffled us why they kept coming even though they didn't seem to appreciate what was on offer. If the seed was growing we didn't see it; if our work was bearing fruit we were certainly not aware of it.

One of the most regular attenders at the group was a young black lad called Paul. He sat quietly in the bay window, often smirking in amusement at the antics of the others. Several years later, I met him at a Christian youthwork conference and discovered that he had become a Christian. He was now a full-time youth worker. He had developed a strong faith and was exercising an important ministry among a very tough group of inner-city kids.

'By the way, Rob,' he whispered, 'did I ever thank you and Jacqui for running that youth group all those years ago? I don't know where I'd have ended up without it.'

Evangelism is often hard, unrewarding and seemingly ineffective, but whenever we sow the seed we must never underestimate the growth that can result. The seeds of the gospel grow quietly, invisibly, steadily – but do not be fooled. The growth is for real.

Sow, even when you're feeling a failure

I once met a young Indian Christian called Augustine. Some years before, he had a dream in which the Lord called him to give up everything and travel to northern India to plant new churches. In simple obedience he sold his home, left his job and moved with his family. He couldn't interest any missionary societies in his vision, but at last two elderly missionary ladies working for the

Elim denomination decided to support him. They themselves had worked in the area for many years, and had found the people hard and unresponsive. They offered hospitality and support to Augustine and his family in the early days of his ministry. Eventually, however, their term of service was over and they returned to England. It was a sad departure, because their combined work had shown no tangible results.

Augustine continued the work, and at last some hardened criminals in a local jail were converted by Christ. Such was the effect of these conversions on the community that many others came to follow Christ. Augustine was able to start a church, and he took teams from this new congregation to evangelise the area. Soon their work led to church groups springing up in many villages. There was still great opposition, but many came to know Jesus Christ as Lord and Saviour.

> **Trying to measure effectiveness in evangelism is a fool's game.**

I first met Augustine when I was visiting the Elim churches' annual conference in Bognor Regis. He was standing at the lectern in the conference hall and speaking to hundreds of British pastors and church leaders. Augustine paid tribute to the faithfulness in prayer and evangelism of those two elderly missionaries, and told everyone that it was they who had sown the seed for the harvest he had reaped. At the same meeting Augustine handed over the title deeds of the twenty churches to the Elim denomination, in recognition of the faithful work of those two missionaries. Their seeming failure in evangelism had in fact been the preparation work for Augustine's 'success'.

Trying to measure effectiveness in evangelism is a fool's game. God – and God alone – brings the increase. When we sow the seed of the gospel, we never know what harvest will one day be reaped. We are called to be faithful rather than successful.

From time to time the Lord does give us a glimpse of the harvest, however, and it can come as a real surprise! I was on the road with an evangelistic presentation called 'Travelling Workshop' when, one night in Salford, my car was broken into and my case stolen. I had to borrow clothes for the next stage of the tour. I felt thoroughly fed up. As my team and I set out for Hull the next morning, it was snowing heavily and the M62 was like a skating rink. The thick snow piled onto the windscreen and the car engine laboured as we motored on through the deepening slush. The three of us who were travelling all had streaming colds and, as a team, we were at an all-time low.

Eventually we found the church where we were to present our evangelistic production. A small audience of thirty arrived and stamped their snowy feet in the hallway, making the entrance dangerously slippery. In the corridor which was our makeshift dressing room, we all groaned. The whole enterprise seemed pointless! We had made a hazardous journey and for what? Thirty people who gave the distinct impression that they wanted our production to finish as soon as possible, since the weather was getting worse. So we cut the presentation short and went to our accommodation feeling rather the worse for wear. There had been no response to the evangelistic challenge and the whole exhausting enterprise seemed like a total waste of effort.

Several years later, when I was speaking at a large student conference in Newcastle, a young woman came up to me and beamed. 'You won't recognise me, but I gave my life to the Lord one night in a blizzard in Hull. Everything's been different since then. I never answered the appeal, but that was the night when I first met Jesus.'

My team and I had felt like pathetic failures that night in Hull. Everything was against us and the work of evangelism seemed a sheer waste of time. But God had other plans. He took the seed we sowed and brought a wonderful increase. To God be the glory, because he did it – not us!

Sow, even when the soil seems hard

When there was nothing to see but bare fields and barren land, Jesus declared, 'I tell you, open your eyes and look at the fields! They are ripe for harvest' (John 4:35). He was looking with the eye of faith. He could see the crop yet to grow, the bountiful harvest yet to be. He could see the distant future, with sower and reaper rejoicing together.

Yes, the field may look barren, but as long as the seed is scattered there is enormous potential for harvest. The one who sows is called not to be successful, only faithful; not to imagine what might have been, only what will surely be; not to make gloomy predictions about the outcome, only to sow in hope. The sower should never feel despondent for, in the providence of God, he or she will surely reap a result.

Sowing has been out of fashion for too long. Those who should have scattered the seed have looked at the barren fields and decided to stay at home. We need the Holy Spirit to give us a new vision for reaching people in the most unlikely situations. But vision doesn't grow through policy meetings; it is something God gives to us as we wait on him and seek his holy will. Jesus commissioned us to go 'into all the world', and not only to sow the seed in what we might consider fertile situations. We are called to sow even in the hard places.

In 1865, no one would have viewed the East End of London as a potential harvest for the kingdom of God. One night, however, William Booth was walking home along Commercial Road when he became overwhelmed by the needs of the people. When he got home he told his wife, 'As I passed by the doors of those gin palaces tonight I seemed to hear a voice saying, "Where can you find such heathen as these, and where is there so great a need for your labours?" I felt as though I ought at all costs to stop and preach to those East End multitudes.'

Booth was a powerful evangelist and a well-known leader in the Methodist Church. Yet he turned his back on it all to respond to the call to go to a 'barren land'. Booth sowed seeds of the gospel in the East End which bore a harvest throughout the world through the ministry of the Salvation Army. Who would have imagined that such a place could have produced a movement of such fervour and compassion?

When I first became a minister, I was overrun with young couples who wanted to get married in the church. The chapel had a very traditional exterior with a tall spire and a pretty garden which people liked 'for the photos'. So the church tended to attract wedding couples for all the wrong reasons. Each week I held wedding interviews and would see as many as three couples in an evening, spending up to an hour with each. During the months before their wedding, I tried to give each couple three interviews in order to get to know them well. The first meeting was very much an introductory session, in which I established a relationship and discussed their plans. The final interview dealt with practical arrangements, and we would talk through the service together. But the second interview was always the most crucial. During this session, I tried to convey something of how faith in Jesus Christ could strengthen and sustain their life together. I hoped that through this some of them might find a faith right at the start of their married life together.

That second interview was always tricky. Sometimes the couple would try to steer the conversation away from anything spiritual and divert the flow to subjects they found more approachable. I often found these marriage preparation talks deeply discouraging. The whole enterprise seemed like 'barren land'.

One couple, however, wanted to know more. They returned again and again to find out more about Jesus. Eventually they gave their lives to Christ. A few years ago I stood in their Yorkshire manse and marvelled at what the Lord had done. Here they were, years later, at the start of their own ministry for Christ. I found it a very emotional experience to talk with them and to hear how they too witness to the couples who come to get married in their church.

We must never write off any soil as barren. It is our task to sow the seed, not predict the outcome. Church history indicates that evangelism in the unlikeliest places and among the most resistant of peoples can bring the biggest harvest of all!

Sow, even when the task seems daunting

A harvest vision sees the gospel as a mustard seed whose growth potential is beyond belief. It sees the gospel as a seed growing silently whose progress cannot be truly measured. It sees the gospel as a seed which, even when planted in the most barren place, can become a mighty harvest. Reflect again on Jesus' parable of the sower and the seed:

> 'Listen! A farmer went out to sow his seed. As he was scattering the seed, some fell along the path, and the birds came and ate it up. Some fell on rocky places, where it did not have much soil. It sprang up quickly, because the soil was shallow But when the sun came up, the plants were scorched, and they withered because they had no root. Other seed fell among thorns, which grew up and choked the plants, so that they did not bear grain. Still other seed fell on good soil. It came up, grew and produced a crop, multiplying thirty, sixty, or even a hundred times.'
> *Mark 4:3–8*

Please note: the story doesn't say, 'A farmer went out to sow – but first he did a statistical return on the prospects of harvest.' Or, 'A farmer went out to sow, but first he conducted a public opinion poll on the political correctness of such an activity.' Or, 'A farmer went out to sow, but first called a committee together to see if they'd give him permission to do so.' No! A sower went out to sow.

If you want a good harvest, don't let a statistician sow the seed. He will stand in the autumn furrow and try to calculate the chances of the seed surviving. He will anticipate chill winds, heavy snows and frozen earth, and forecast a poor harvest if any harvest at all. As the writer of Ecclesiastes observed, 'Whoever watches the wind will not plant; whoever looks at the clouds will not reap.'

If you want a good harvest, don't use a pollster to sow the seed. He will stand, opinion poll in one hand and calculator in the other, and compute the chances of a crop. He has canvassed public opinion and decided that harvests aren't popular any more. He has examined the complex food markets of the world and concluded there's insufficient demand. So he recommends that harvest be cancelled this year.

If you want a good harvest, don't ask a committee to sow the seed. They will stand at the edge of the field muttering disapprovingly to each other and protecting their pristine green wellingtons from the mud. Committees cannot sow without a majority and, as they rarely agree on anything, majorities are hard to find. They will conclude that the soil is poor and the prospects bleak. Perhaps next year...

If you want a good harvest, don't employ an agricultural expert to sow the seed. His diploma in soil management, degree in farm technology and doctorate in agrarian history have not prepared him for such a task. He sits at his computer and produces colour graphs projecting the failure of the crop, but he never sows seed himself. He never ventures out into the field or feels the rich dark soil running through his fingers. His thesis argues that harvests are a thing of the past. Sowing seed is no longer worth the effort.

But somewhere, a sower goes out to sow. He barely understands the process, let alone the depressing theoretical predictions of the experts. He throws the raw seed into the gusting wind and his heart is full of hope. He is driven by a conviction too deep for words and he knows that, against all odds, harvest will surely come.

Sowing must be done by those who are committed to the task and who know that, out of their faithfulness, the harvest will surely come. Sadly, 'the harvest is plentiful but the workers are few.' Pray that the Lord of the harvest will send out others to join in this work. Pray that he will open the eyes of many in our churches today to see this vision and to know the privilege and joy of becoming sowers of the seed.

APPENDICES

These appendices are offered as tools to help you in your church mission. Adapt them freely to suit your community and church context.

Appendix 1

Taking an audit of church life

1 What kind of church do we represent?

How many demonstrate commitment by church membership or tithing?

What is our average congregation in the morning? In the evening?

What midweek meetings are there, if any?

Are they mainly inward-focused or outward-focused?

Do we have a Sunday school, or other children's groups?

Is there a women's fellowship?

Are there any house groups?

What is the average age of the congregation?

Do we have any young families?

Have we received any new members in recent months?

2 In what ways does our church interface with the local community?

How do we view ourselves?

Do we feel we have become a clique?

How do others see us?

Do we regularly bring friends and colleagues to see what's happening?

Are there regular 'ways in' to the church such as special guest events?

Are there opportunities for people to hear about Jesus and respond to him?

Are there natural ways to follow up those who come to faith?

Have there been any new converts recently?

Are there new signs of faith and witness?

Are our members effective witnesses?

Do we provide training in evangelism?

Do we have a vision for growth?

Does our church function more for its members or for those outside the life of the church?

Are we welcoming and friendly?

3 What kind of area are we working in?

Do many people commute?

What industry are most people in the area involved in?

Are there many retired people?

Are there many teenagers or children in the area?

Are there belts of new housing?

What significant changes, if any, are happening to the character and constituency of people in our catchment area?

Have people moved into the congregation as newcomers to the area? If not, why not?

4 What kind of mission outreach are other churches nearby doing?

Should we be working with them?

How can we be partners in mission yet avoid competition?

What kind of ecumenical relationships do we have?

Is there a church of a different denomination nearby?

Do we have united services with another church regularly? Occasionally? Never?

Would it be good for the mission to be an ecumenical venture?

Is the other vicar/minister supportive of our work?

5 How have things been going recently?

Has our youth work grown or declined?

Have we had an influx of new children in the Sunday School?

Are we particularly concerned about the numbers of ageing church members?

Are some of our stalwarts moving away?

Have any groups or organisations recently closed down? Started up?

How is the spiritual life of the church?

Is there any need for renewal of the prayer life in the church?

Have there been any evangelistic outreach activities in recent years?

Have we received any new members in recent months?

Have we any particular things within the life of our church that we are particularly excited about?

6 How do we think the visiting mission team could help us in the ongoing life and witness of our church?

Should we:

Restart or strengthen children's work?

Start a youth fellowship?

Visit people in the area?

Make contact with local schools?

Train new local leaders in evangelism?

Encourage the prayer life of members in the church?

Make contact with people on the church's community roll?

Attempt to reach those who are totally outside the orbit of the church?

Make contact with those who have recently moved into the community?

7 Looking at our ideas from 6, in what ways do we think our church could prepare for a mission team?

What facilities do we have (or not have) in the church that might be important in planning a mission (eg kitchen/ toilets/ team rooms)?

What local hospitality/ sleeping accommodation/ catering can be offered to the visiting team?

8 In what ways could the church follow up the work of the mission?

Form a nurture group for new converts?

Provide teachers for a new Sunday School or children's club?

Run a new prayer group or home group?

Appendix 2

Carrying out a survey of the local community

Age

Sex

Occupation

Do you work locally?

How long have you lived in the area?

Do you talk to your neighbours, or visit them?

What sort of neighbourhood is this? How would you describe it?

What are the main problems in this area?

What facilities are lacking in this area?

Who would you look to help you in a time of crisis?

Where would you recommend people go to if they wanted to meet new friends? Get help or advice? Have a good time?

Do you belong to any groups in this area?

Where do you meet people socially around here?

Do you attend church?

Do you know anyone who does?

What is your impression of the local churches?

What would you like to see the churches doing in this area?

Preparing a church vision statement

A church may wish to use the following agenda after the completion of a community survey. It is designed to move the church towards creating its own vision statement.

What new opportunities for witness have we identified within our community? What new people groups have we found?

What local needs have we found and how can we meet them?

Do we need to relocate our work to where the people are?

Do we need to develop forms of worship which are more culturally relevant to the groups identified?

What is our strategy for evangelism in our area?

How can we make initial contact with the target community?

How can we engage people in that group in a serious consideration of Christian faith?

How can we encourage a firm commitment to Christ and disciple new converts?

Should we begin public worship in this newly identified area and, if so, how can we train up new local leaders?

Do we need to become more down-market and approachable?

Do we believe that God has a future for our church?

Appendix 4

Setting goals for local mission

Typical goals could be:

- To contact new families who have moved into the area and spend time with them.
- To start or work with a parent and toddler group.
- To work in local schools with the aim of strengthening the church's youth programme.
- To start a series of home groups or Alpha groups.
- To contact lapsed church members.
- To spend time with the elderly, the housebound and the sick.
- To work with the unemployed or with other groups who may feel alienated from the community.

An example of real working goals taken from a mission (Catalyst, held in Hastings in August 2007):

- To share the gospel with skaters.
- To show God's love through acts of service.
- To launch a youth church in Ore Valley.
- To kick-start a holiday club in Silverhill.
- To build links between the Greater Hollington Forum and the local churches.
- To invite 300 people to the next Big Bang event.
- To pray with 30 people in the town centre.
- To level a sports field so it can be used again.

The programme for Catalyst Hastings was built around six areas with possible projects for each:

Acts of kindness – giving away coffee or ice cream; serving people with practical offers of everything from washing-up to ironing or gardening.

Community sports – local tournaments featuring football, skateboarding, 10-pin bowling etc, with prizegivings and celebrations; family sports days; training classes.

Using the arts – exhibitions by local Christian artists; large murals; flower festival; junk model day; dance, drama and music workshops; talent contest.

Ecological projects – 'green' mission – cleaning up a community area; creating a local nature reserve or planting flowers; seting up a recycling depot; fundraising for local charities.

Community service – working in urban priority areas on home decorating; visiting the housebound; holding a community barbecue; working with other racial groups to provide an evening of different ethnic foods.

Christian spirituality – setting up local prayer stations; offering classes on meditation etc.

Here is a checklist of suggestions for other types of activity that you might like to consider for your mission:

School assemblies and classroom presentations
Christian apologetics evenings (eg the science and faith debate)
Community conferences on global issues
Music celebrations and concerts
Flower festivals, maybe using a biblical theme
Games evenings with interviews of Christian sportsmen and women
Pilgrimages to historic Christian sites
Sponsored events with visitors and locals participating
Pub meetings, with seminars or discussions
'Colour me Beautiful' programmes for women
Workshops on subjects such as handling stress, parenting or bereavement
Barbecues, picnics and banquets
Evangelistic preaching